the VERMONT FARM TABLE COOKBOOK

the VERMONT FARM TABLE COOKBOOK

Homegrown Recipes from the Green Mountain State

TRACEY MEDEIROS

Photographs by OLIVER PARINI

Countryman Press

An Imprint of W. W. Norton & Company
Celebrating a Century of Independent Publishing

For information about permission to reproduce selections from
this book, write to Permissions, Countryman Press, 500 Fifth
Avenue, New York, NY 10110

For information about special discounts for bulk purchases,
please contact W. W. Norton Special Sales at specialsales@
wwnorton.com or 800-233-4830

Manufacturing by Versa Press
Production manager: Devon Zahn

Countryman Press
www.countrymanpress.com

An imprint of W. W. Norton & Company, Inc.
500 Fifth Avenue, New York, NY 10110
www.wwnorton.com

978-1-68268-807-6 (pbk)

10 9 8 7 6 5 4 3 2 1

I dedicate this book to my beautiful son, Peter, my nephews, Mason and Maxwell, and my niece, Lillian. You inspire my passion for a healthier planet.

CONTENTS

ACKNOWLEDGMENTS

My hope is that the profiles, recipes, and photographs in this book have put a face to the hardworking people who so very generously helped to make *The Vermont Farm Table Cookbook* an appetizing reality. A heartfelt thank-you to all of the farmers, chefs, and food producers who work endlessly toward the common goal of building and maintaining healthy soil, which produces wholesome, sustainable foods that feed and promote wellness for communities. This book would not have been possible without you.

Thank you to the entire team at Countryman Press—including former editorial director, Kermit Hummel, who gave me the chance to bring this book to life. Many thanks to Ann Treistman and Isabel McCarthy for offering me the wonderful opportunity to revise the cookbook. Oliver Parini, my very talented photographer, for his beautiful images and helping to create a stunning book. To my recipes testers, Pamela Cohan, Justin Molson, and Sarah Strauss, for generously offering your feedback and for making sure that each contributor's recipe delivers. Finally, I must thank my caring husband, Peter, mother, Sheridan, and sister, Kelley, who make me believe that all things are possible. I am grateful for your undying support. Thank you.

A portion of the proceeds from the sale of this book will be donated to the Vermont Foodbank.

INTRODUCTION: A GASTRONOMIC PORTRAIT OF THE GREEN MOUNTAIN STATE

Vermont has long been considered the epicenter of all foods good and wholesome. This picturesque state of rolling farmlands and breathtaking mountain vistas offers a wonderful diversity of agriculture on its sprawling, earthy canvas. Bustling farmers' markets and community-supported farms provide direct access to fresh, locally grown products. They bolster the state's agricultural philosophy of bringing the food to the people, knowing the source of your food, and supporting the local food chain.

The farm-to-table cycle has long been a way of life in Vermont, part of the ethos that Vermonters use to define themselves. It is with a sense of accomplishment and pride that we joyfully celebrate the 10th anniversary of *The Vermont Farm Table Cookbook*. During the past decade, the love for the Green Mountain State and its farmers, chefs, and food producers has remained unwavering. This anniversary edition is a culinary tribute to their resilience and love of community.

It is with a heavy heart that I have had to say farewell to some of the hardworking people featured in the first edition of this cookbook. This revised version will introduce readers to a dozen exciting new contributors and two dozen fresh, wholesome recipes that will be sure to hasten your family to the table. The book demonstrates the importance of community and its support for local businesses and farms. Readers will be pleased to see the return of over 65 familiar names from the original cookbook, learning how their businesses and farming ventures have, in some cases, been refashioned to meet the changing times.

Each recipe in this cookbook is an edible story. Some are culinary heirlooms, handed down from generation to generation, while other contributors have skillfully created their own. I am delighted to once again welcome Darby Farm in Alburgh, to our 10th anniversary edition. The couple's certified organic farm has been in the Darby family for over 200 years. Heather Darby and her husband, Ron, operate this seventh-generation farm, which also carries on the Darby's legacy of beekeeping. High Ridge Meadow Farm, nestled in the hills of East Randolph, is owned by Mary and Jim Moran. This hardworking couple considers it an honor to continue the state's legacy of farming.

Simon Pearce has generously supported and carried the cookbook in their stores throughout these many years. Their award-winning restaurant, located at the flagship store in Quechee, Vermont, is a shining example of the farm-to-table movement. By sourcing from local and regional farms and food producers, they not only support the local community, but our state as well. Each of their beautiful pieces of glassware and pottery is a masterpiece of craftsmanship.

As Vermont continues to be a pioneer in the farm-to-table movement, I am pleased to welcome newcomer, Honey Road, to the cookbook community. This women-owned enterprise believes in buying local, thereby supporting the area's small farms and businesses. It is with pleasure that Moon and Stars Arepas joins the ranks of the new cookbook contributors. Nando Jaramillo, its creator, is working to expand the sustainable farming of heirloom corn varieties. It is his dream to revitalize organic heirloom corn. The Good Food Foundation's judges have awarded Jaramillo's arepas with their 2022 award of excellence in "Grains."

Vermont, like the rest of our country, has weathered a variety of ups and downs during the past 10 years. Life as we know it has changed to some degree yet, through it all, the Green Mountain State remains true to its mission of preserving their agricultural system. On August 2, 2022, Governor Phil Scott proclaimed August as "Agritourism Month" in Vermont. Agritourism introduces visitors to the farming community offering them a way to learn about the farming way of life. Whether it be a farm tour or dinner, hayride, pick-your-own orchard or farm festival, these occasions provide the public with hands-on educational opportunities. Each farm is unique, offering its guests a variety of experiences and products. This generates revenue which allows small and mid-sized farms to remain competitive, helping to preserve Vermont's agricultural landscape.

By supporting the local food chain, it not only enriches the well-being of Vermont's farming community but

ensures its preservation for years to come. Buying local secures the economic health of the state's agricultural system. Preserving the state's farms enables consumers to have access to fresh, locally grown products and a healthier way of life. Farmers' markets, restaurants, and local businesses also benefit, helping to bolster Vermont's economy. The ensuing effect is a win for all.

Small, independent farms are the lifeblood of Vermont's agricultural system. The Green Mountain State's enduring respect for the land, and desire to use it in the most productive way possible, has made Vermont a respected role model, both nationally and internationally. Their emphasis is on environmental health while still maintaining economic profitability. The state's productive food system recognizes the importance of community, realizing that the bond between farmers and consumers is what makes Vermont truly unique. This state raises the bar when it comes to preserving their agricultural way of life and support of the area's business community. Buying local is a source of pride for Vermonters.

Showcasing Vermont's bounty gives me a great sense of satisfaction and it is the driving force behind this carefully curated, gastronomic portrait of the Green Mountain State. It is my hope that the collection of rustic-yet-refined Vermont inspired recipes and heartwarming stories featured in this updated edition will capture your interest and whet your appetite for more, as you embark on a culinary exploration of our beautiful state. As Vermonters, we look to the past with a sense of nostalgia and to the future with enthusiasm, determination, and hope.

Nathaniel Hawthorne so eloquently said, "Time flies over us, but leaves its shadow behind." With the past as our guide, what we do with today will pave the way for a brighter tomorrow. Come, join us on this unforgettable journey!

BREADS

Rory's Irish Scones

MAKES 54 SMALL SCONES

Friends of the Simon Pearce family, Darina and Tim Allen own and operate the esteemed Ballymaloe Cookery School in Shanagarry, Ireland; this quick and easy recipe is from Darina's brother, chef Rory O'Connell. At Simon Pearce's restaurant, they make these scones using King Arthur unbleached bread flour. Serve these scones with soups, salads, or main courses; they are perfect any time. See photo on page 15.

4 cups bread flour, plus extra for rolling

½ heaping teaspoon baking soda

1 teaspoon salt

½ heaping teaspoon granulated sugar

2 cups buttermilk

1. Preheat the oven to 400°F. Lightly flour a baking sheet and set aside.

2. Sift the flour, baking soda, salt, and sugar into a large mixing bowl. Make a well in the center of the dry mixture and add the buttermilk. Mix together by hand until thoroughly combined. (Be careful not to overwork the dough; it should be light and springy to the touch.)

3. Turn the dough out onto a well-floured surface and form into a large rectangle. Using a rolling pin and extra flour as needed, roll the dough into a 9 x 6-inch rectangle about ¾ inch thick.

4. Cut the dough into 9 strips about 1 inch wide, then cut each of the strips into six 1-inch squares.

5. Arrange the dough squares on the prepared baking sheet in nine rows of six, so they are just barely touching. (As they rise in the oven, the scones will merge together.) Bake until the scones are golden brown, 17 to 20 minutes, rotating the baking sheet halfway through the baking time. Let the scones cool on the baking sheet for 5 minutes, then remove them from the sheet and gently separate them before serving.

Simon Pearce

TYLER PLACE FAMILY RESORT

Located on a mile of private lakeshore on Lake Champlain, the Tyler Place Family Resort is surrounded by natural beauty. Since 1933, this Vermont country inn has been offering all-inclusive family vacations and is rated among the top 10 family-friendly destination resorts in the United States.

Local foods are the key to their menu. The Tyler Place is committed to supporting local purveyors of fresh products. The chef, kitchen staff, and food manager seek out the best the area has to offer, from local dairies to vegetable growers, creameries to smokehouses.

Crème Brûlée French Toast

SERVES 6 TO 8

4 cups half-and-half

1 cup pure Vermont maple syrup

3 large eggs, lightly beaten

1½ teaspoons vanilla extract

2 loaves challah bread, sliced ¾ to 1 inch thick, slices cut in half

8 tablespoons (4 ounces) unsalted butter

1 cup packed light brown sugar

Confectioners' sugar

1. Lightly grease two 9 x 13-inch baking pans. In a large bowl, whisk together the half-and-half, maple syrup, eggs, and vanilla. Place the bread slices in a single layer in the prepared pans. Divide the custard mixture between the two pans, pouring it evenly over the bread, and press on the bread to allow it to absorb the liquid. Cover with plastic wrap and refrigerate overnight.

2. Preheat the oven to 350°F. Cover the pans with foil and bake until the custard is set, 25 to 30 minutes. Remove from the oven and let cool slightly.

3. Meanwhile, combine the butter and brown sugar in a small saucepan over medium-low heat and cook, whisking occasionally, until the butter is melted and the sugar is dissolved.

4. Drizzle the French toast with the brown sugar mixture, dust with confectioners' sugar, if desired, and serve.

Tyler Place Family Resort

KING ARTHUR BAKING COMPANY

Founded in 1790, King Arthur Baking Company is the oldest flour company in America. The bakery, baking education center, café, and store are located in Norwich. King Arthur Baking Company's fundamental mission is to support and seek to expand all aspects of baking by being the highest quality product, information, and education resource for, and inspiration to, bakers worldwide. The company has been employee-owned since 1996.

Ingredients	Weight	Baker's Percentage
Sifted whole-wheat pastry flour	.545 kg	100%
Sugar	.136 kg	25%
Baking powder	.032 kg	6%
Salt	.003 kg	.5%
Butter, cold	.136 kg	25%
Currants	.109 kg	20%
Heavy cream	290 kg	53.1%
Buttermilk	205 kg	37.5%
Eggs, large	1 (.06 kg)	11%

Currant Scones

MAKES 12 TO 14 SCONES

These scones are in the Irish style—moist, rich, and light. They are made daily at the King Arthur Baking Company on-site bakery. Cranberries can substitute nicely for the currants, or the dried fruit can be omitted entirely.

4⅓ cups sifted whole-wheat pastry flour

½ cup plus 1 tablespoon granulated sugar

3 tablespoons baking powder

½ teaspoon salt

8 tablespoons (4 ounces) unsalted butter, cut into small pieces

1 cup dried currants or cranberries

1 cup plus 3 tablespoons heavy cream

1 cup buttermilk

1 large egg

1. Preheat the oven to 425°F. Spray a baking sheet with nonstick cooking spray and set aside.

2. Using a stand mixer fitted with the paddle attachment, mix together the flour, sugar, baking powder, and salt. Add the butter and beat on low speed until the mixture forms pea-sized lumps. Add the currants and mix just until combined.

3. In a small bowl, whisk together the cream, buttermilk, and egg. Add to the dry mixture and stir by hand just until combined.

4. Using a ½-cup scoop, portion the dough onto the prepared baking sheet. Bake until the tops are slightly springy, 15 to 18 minutes. Serve warm.

Note: If desired, in step 4, whisk 1 large egg with 2 tablespoons milk or water and brush over the tops of the scones before baking them.

King Arthur Baking Company

Nana's Caraway Seed Biscuits

MAKES ABOUT 18 BISCUITS

These biscuits come from Mary Moran, owner of High Ridge Meadows Farm in East Randolph. Moran's grandmother taught her how to make caraway seed biscuits many years ago. Her grandmother would make them for the extended family every week, never measuring the ingredients; just a handful of this and a pinch of that. You can use between 2 and 3 tablespoons of caraway seeds, depending on how "seedy" you like your biscuits. They are delicious and easy to make; serve them alongside a hearty meal or on their own, with butter and a drizzle of honey, if desired.

¼ cup shortening, lard, or unsalted butter

2½ cups whole milk

1 tablespoon granulated sugar

2 tablespoons active dry yeast

5 cups all-purpose flour, or as needed

2–3 tablespoons caraway seeds

2 teaspoons salt

1. Melt the shortening in a medium saucepan over medium heat. Add the milk and sugar and heat until very warm, about 110°F. Remove from the heat and add the yeast. Let stand for 2 minutes or until bubbles begin to form.

2. Combine the flour, caraway seeds, and salt in a large bowl. Stir in the yeast mixture until a soft dough forms. Cover with a damp dishcloth and let rise in a warm place until the dough doubles in volume, about 45 minutes.

3. Preheat the oven to 375°F. Lightly grease a baking sheet. Roll the dough out and cut with a 2-inch biscuit cutter, or simply tear pieces off with your fingers and form biscuits. Place the biscuits on the prepared baking sheet. Cover with a damp dishcloth and let rise a second time in a warm place, just enough to have them spring back, about 30 minutes. Transfer to the oven and bake until golden brown, about 20 minutes. Serve.

High Ridge Meadows Farm

TWO BLACK SHEEP FARM

Two Black Sheep Farm, located in South Hero, Vermont, is dedicated to small scale organic vegetable production. It was started in 1992 by three farmers—Kurt and Deborah Sherman, along with their son-in-law, Erik Van Hauer. Currently there are two partners, Erik having moved on to his own farming enterprise in Marshfield, Vermont.

Two Black Sheep is located on just under three acres of land with about a half-acre under till, as well as a hoop house for cold-weather vegetable production. The farm's two Romney sheep, Nellie and Olive, keep production going when the farmers lag. The barn cat, Joanie, takes care of the birds who would like to reside there, while the family's dog, Angus, has an eternal wish to let Joanie know who really is boss! Although, the farm ceased offering CSA shares in 2019, a farm stand on the property does brisk sales. As part of their summer experience, folks vacationing in South Hero look forward to shopping at the stand.

The farm enjoys a great deal of patronage because of the summer's tomato, pepper, and eggplant harvest. Corn, pumpkins, and Brussels sprouts follow, with the stand closing the beginning of November. In November and December, Two Black Sheep also offers wreaths and swags as a value-added product. These are always sought-after items because of their artistic flair and thrifty pricing. They are crafted by the owners' daughter, Courtney.

Zucchini Bread

MAKES 2 LOAVES

The zucchini bread recipe came from Kurt Sherman's grandmother, Hetty Sherman. When he first made this bread, Kurt didn't know the difference between "dice," "chop," and "purée" so he wound up puréeing the zucchini instead of shredding it. The accidental result produced a loaf of bread that the entire family found appealing. Sherman has baked these zucchini loaves on many special occasions and once made 120 loaves in a single day, as favors to be given to guests attending his daughter and son-in-law's wedding. (Fortunately, he had some help from the groom-to-be.)

3 large eggs, lightly beaten

1 cup canola or vegetable oil

1 tablespoon vanilla extract

3 cups all-purpose flour

2 cups granulated sugar

1 tablespoon ground cinnamon

1 teaspoon grated nutmeg

1 teaspoon sea salt

1 teaspoon baking soda

½ teaspoon baking powder

2 cups puréed unpeeled zucchini

1 cup raisins, chopped walnuts, or
    chocolate chips (optional)

1. Preheat the oven to 350°F. Spray two 9 x 5-inch loaf pans with nonstick cooking spray and lightly dust with flour. Set aside.

2. Whisk together the eggs, oil, and vanilla.

3. Sift together the flour, sugar, cinnamon, nutmeg, sea salt, baking soda, and baking powder. Add the flour mixture to the wet ingredients and stir until smooth. Stir in the zucchini and raisins, nuts, or chocolate chips, if using. Pour into the prepared loaf pans and bake until a toothpick inserted into the center of the bread comes out clean, about 1 hour.

4. Let the bread cool in the pans for about 15 minutes, then turn the loaves out onto a cooling rack. Let cool completely before serving.

Two Black Sheep Farm

Hungarian Nokedli (Dumplings)

SERVES 4

Pitchfork Farm is a 30-acre organic vegetable farm located at the Intervale in Burlington, Vermont. The co-owners, Eric Seitz and Rob Rock, grow over 30 varieties of crops. The partners are committed to growing only the highest quality fresh produce to sustain themselves, the land, and the community. These dumplings, from Seitz's grandmother, are a superb complement to Chicken Paprika (page 120).

Kosher salt

2 cups all-purpose flour

2 large eggs, lightly beaten

½ cup water, plus extra as needed

1 tablespoon unsalted butter

Grated Parmesan cheese

Chopped fresh parsley

1. Bring 3 quarts water and 1 tablespoon salt to a boil in a large saucepan. In a medium bowl, stir together the flour and ½ teaspoon salt. Make a well, add the eggs and water, and stir until a wet and sticky dough begins to form. (If necessary, add more water so that the dough is soft enough to press through a spaetzle maker.)

2. Working in batches, press the dough through a spaetzle maker and add the dumplings to the boiling water. Cook until the dumplings float to the surface, about 2 minutes per batch. Scoop out with a small sieve or slotted spoon. Transfer to a large bowl.

3. Toss the spaetzle with the butter and Parmesan and season with salt to taste. Garnish with parsley. Serve.

Note: If you don't have a spaetzle maker, push the dough through the largest holes of a box grater.

Pitchfork Farm

Caribbean Cornbread

MAKES 15 TO 18 PIECES

Conant's uses Early Riser Cornmeal from Butter-works Farm in this cornbread. If you can't find it, use any good whole-grain cornmeal.

1 cup all-purpose flour

1 cup cornmeal

2 tablespoons baking soda

¾ cup granulated sugar

1 teaspoon kosher salt

16 tablespoons (8 ounces) unsalted butter, melted

4 large eggs, lightly beaten

1½ cups fresh corn kernels and juice
    (cut from about 2 ears corn)

½ cup crushed pineapple, drained well

4 ounces mild or sharp cheddar
    cheese, shredded (1 cup)

1. Preheat the oven to 350°F. Spray a 9 x 13-inch baking pan with nonstick cooking spray and set aside.

2. In a large bowl, combine the flour, cornmeal, baking soda, sugar, and salt. In a medium bowl, whisk together the butter and eggs. Fold in the corn with its juice, pineapple, and ¾ cup of the cheddar cheese. Make a well in the center of the dry ingredients and pour in the wet mixture. Stir until just combined.

3. Pour the batter into the prepared pan and smooth with a spatula. Sprinkle the remaining ¼ cup cheese over the top. Bake until golden brown and a tooth-pick inserted into the center comes out clean, 35 to 40 minutes.

Conant's Riverside Farm/Riverside Produce

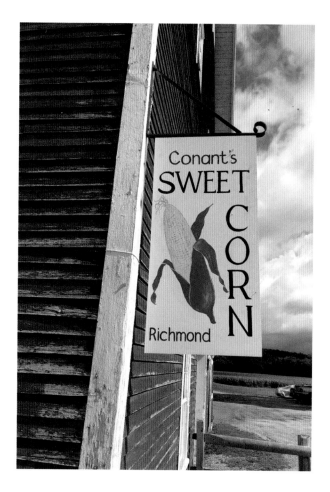

BHAKTA 50 SPIRITS

When American entrepreneur Raj Bhakta acquired the Armagnac brandy division from the French company, Maison Ryst-Dupeyron, he prepared to embark on yet another exciting chapter in his life. Armagnac is a highly aromatic grape brandy, originating in the French region of Gascony. It is believed to be among the oldest and finest distilled spirits in the world, smooth and complex in flavor. Maison Ryst-Dupeyron was known to have one of the oldest and largest stocks of this regional brandy, which dates as far back as the mid-19th century.

After acquisition negotiations were successfully completed, Bhakta began shipping the precious cargo back to his farm in Vermont. He has now reinvented this category of brandy by creating his own brand, BHAKTA 50. A glass of this magnificently aged brandy, with its 100 percent antique French Armagnacs, is reminiscent of another time and place. Raj Bhakta envisions creating the finest spirits by reviving their forgotten flavors and elegant, sophisticated taste.

The brand's eye-catching label, BHAKTA 50, is designed to inform brandy aficionados of the fact that none of the Armagnacs used in its blends are less than 50 years old. History tells us that the oldest were distilled as early as 1868. The beautifully designed bottle with its clean, graceful lines speaks to the contents within, a combination of unique tasting vintages that distinguish this brandy from its peers.

Constantly creating new business opportunities, Bhakta has planted vineyards and grain on his farm in Shoreham, Vermont. He has recently purchased an apple orchard in the Champlain Valley; its fruit will be used to make an apple brandy. The busy spirits entrepreneur realizes that BHAKTA 50 will, at some point, transition to a modern American brandy. Before this occurs, it is his hope that spirit connoisseurs will take notice of and appreciate this exquisite line of brandy that has survived the test of time. In the interim, Raj Bhakta is busy introducing brandy lovers to his new line of spirits, lovingly stored in sophisticated, handsome bottles that bear his name.

Brioche

MAKES 2 (8 X 4-INCH) LOAVES

This classic French bread has a soft interior and tender crumb. This homemade brioche is deliciously rich and buttery and pairs beautifully with mushrooms and cream. See page 106 for the Brioche aux Champignons recipe.

    This recipe produces two loaves, and you will only need one loaf for the Brioche aux Champignons. Reserve the second loaf for brunch and serve with whipped butter and your favorite jam or use for French toast.

Sponge

1 package active dry yeast (about 2¼ teaspoons)

¼ cup slightly warm water (approximately 100°F)

¾ cup organic bread flour

¼ cup sugar

2 tablespoons brandy, such as BHAKTA 27-07 Brandy

Dough

5 large free-range organic egg plus 2 egg yolks

1 pound (just under 4 cups) organic bread flour

2 teaspoons fleur de sel

1 pound (4 sticks) organic grass-fed unsalted butter, sliced into 2-tablespoon cubes, softened (approximately 75°F)

Egg Wash

1 large egg yolk, lightly beaten

1 tablespoon water

1. To make the sponge: In the bowl of a stand mixer fitted with a paddle attachment, add the yeast and water and whisk on low speed to combine. Let the yeast sit until it becomes frothy and bubbly, about 10 minutes. Add the flour, sugar, and brandy and mix on medium speed until gooey and supple. Cover tightly with plastic wrap and let rise in a warm corner of the kitchen (75°F) until the dough has doubled in bulk, about 1¼ to 2 hours, depending on the warmth of your kitchen.

2. To make the dough: When the sponge has doubled in bulk, add the 5 eggs plus 2 yolks, flour, and fleur de sel. Using the dough hook, beat on low speed for 10 minutes. With the mixer running on low speed, add the butter, 2 tablespoons at a time, letting each piece incorporate before adding the next. Repeat until all the butter has been incorporated into the dough.

3. Turn the dough out onto a clean, lightly floured surface, carefully folding it over several times. Transfer to a greased bowl large enough for the dough to double in size. Cover tightly with plastic wrap and let the dough double in size on the counter, punching down with your fingers to deflate, about 2 hours and 30 minutes. Cover again with plastic wrap and refrigerate for 20 hours.

4. To make the brioche: Butter two 8 x 4-inch loaf pans and set aside. Turn the dough out onto a lightly floured surface and gently knead for a few minutes to deflate. Remove two small pieces of dough, form into small oblongs, and place them in a buttered dish then cover with plastic wrap and set aside. Divide the remaining dough into two equal portions and form them into loaf shapes that fit neatly into the pans, barely touching the inside walls then cover with plastic wrap. Set aside and allow the loaves and dough oblongs to proof until they have doubled in size, about 3 hours.

5. Using a spatula, gently lay the dough oblongs on top and into the center of each loaf. You do not need to dent the tops of the loaves, just lay the oblongs on top and let them settle in with their own weight.

6. Preheat the oven to 350°F.

7. To make the egg wash: While the oven is pre-heating, whisk together the egg and water in a small bowl.

8. Brush the dough with the egg wash and bake for about 55 minutes, or until an instant-read thermometer registers at 190°F. Let rest on a cooling rack for 1 hour. To unmold: Run a thin-bladed knife, around the outside edges of the loaves to loosen them from the pans. Gently invert the pans onto a wire rack and allow the breads to continue to cool to room temperature before slicing.

9. Serve with the mushroom sauce found on page 106.

Note: You will need to start the brioche at least 2 days before you intend to use it for the Brioche aux Champignons (page 106).

Chef Philip Davis for BHAKTA 50 Spirits

CABOT CREAMERY CO-OPERATIVE

Cabot Creamery Co-operative has made the world's finest dairy products using only the freshest ingredients for over a century. Their award-winning cheeses, yogurts, sour cream, cottage cheese, and butter stand apart because of Cabot farmers' tireless dedication to quality. From being named the "World's Best Cheddar" to becoming the world's first dairy co-operative to achieve B-Corp status, Cabot is owned by dedicated farm families throughout New England and upstate New York. Cabot employs more than 1,000 people and operates three cheese production facilities in Vermont and New York, plus a butter production facility in Massachusetts.

Farmhouse Cheddar Poutine

SERVES 4

We've taken this traditional French-Canadian classic and given it our own Cabot twist. We tossed the oven-roasted red potatoes with crumbly pieces of Cabot Farmhouse Reserve Cheddar Cheese, then generously spooned rich brown gravy all over the potatoes and cheese, and garnished with scallions over the top. You can also serve poutine over toast using Brioche (page 24).

Potatoes

2 pounds red skinned potatoes, cut into bite-sized wedges

1 tablespoon avocado oil or organic canola oil

½ teaspoon salt blend, such as Jane's Krazy Mixed-Up Salt, or to taste

¼ teaspoon freshly ground black pepper, or to taste

Gravy

3 tablespoons unsalted butter

3 tablespoons all-purpose flour

½ cup milk

½ cup beef broth

1½ teaspoons wheat-free tamari, liquid aminos, or soy sauce, or to taste

1 teaspoon Worcestershire sauce

1 teaspoon ketchup

For Serving

6 ounces Cabot Farmhouse Reserve Cheddar Cheese, cut into small crumbly pieces using a flat cheese knife

2–3 scallions, sliced on the diagonal, green parts only

1. Preheat the oven to 400°F. Generously grease a baking sheet with oil. Set aside.

2. To make the roasted potatoes: Place the potatoes, oil, salt, and pepper in a large bowl, tossing until well combined. Spread the potatoes out in a single layer onto the prepared baking sheet and roast, stirring once, until the potatoes are fork tender and slightly browned, about 35 minutes, depending on the size of the wedges.

3. While the potatoes are roasting, make the gravy. Melt the butter in a small saucepan over medium heat, swirling the saucepan occasionally until golden browned. Remove from the heat, add the flour 1 tablespoon at a time, whisking continuously until you have a smooth paste. In a slow and steady stream, vigorously whisk in the milk, broth, tamari, Worcestershire sauce, and ketchup. Return the saucepan to the heat, increase to medium-high and bring to a simmer, whisking continuously, until gravy is smooth and thick. Add additional Worcestershire sauce and ketchup, if desired.

4. To serve: Divide the potatoes and cheese among four plates. Lightly season with salt and pepper and toss until well combined. Generously spoon the gravy over and around the potatoes and cheese. Garnish with scallions and serve immediately.

Katie Webster for Cabot Creamery Co-operative

Vegan Chili

SERVES 6 TO 8

This chili is so popular at the City Market, Onion River Co-op that it is served in the deli every day of the week. Many farms in Vermont grow dried beans, which you can easily substitute for the canned beans in this recipe; you will need 1½ cups cooked kidney beans and 2½ cups cooked black beans. Vary the amount of jalapeños you add to suit your taste. See photo on page 27.

1 tablespoon sunflower oil

1 medium yellow onion, diced (about ¾ cup)

1 cup shredded carrots

1–2 jalapeño peppers, stemmed, seeded,
    and minced (about 3 tablespoons)

3 garlic cloves, minced

½ cup bulgur, rinsed

2 tablespoons chili powder

1 tablespoon ground cumin

2 cups diced fresh tomatoes (about 2 medium
    or 6 plum tomatoes)

1½ cups tomato sauce

1 (15-ounce) can kidney beans, drained and rinsed

1½ (15-ounce) cans black beans, drained and rinsed

1½ teaspoons kosher salt, or to taste

Vegetable stock (optional; see Note)

Organic vegan sour cream (optional)

Chopped fresh cilantro (optional)

1. Heat the oil in a Dutch oven or large heavy pot over medium-high heat. Add the onion, carrots, and jalapeño and sauté, stirring often, until the onion is soft and translucent, about 5 minutes. Add the garlic and sauté for 1 minute. Add the bulgur, chili powder, and cumin and stir until well combined.

2. Stir in the tomatoes, tomato sauce, and beans. Bring to a boil, then reduce the heat, cover, and simmer, stirring every 10 to 15 minutes, scraping the bottom of the pot to prevent sticking, until the beans are tender, about 1 hour. Season with salt to taste. Serve with a dollop of sour cream and a sprinkling of cilantro, if desired.

Note: Depending on the ripeness of your tomatoes, you may need to add 1 to 2 tablespoons of vegetable stock to help prevent the chili from sticking to the bottom of the pot.

City Market, Onion River Co-op

ARCANA GARDENS AND GREENHOUSES

Arcana Gardens and Greenhouses is a 140-acre certified organic farm with retail greenhouses, located east of Burlington, in Jericho. Most of the plants sold at Arcana are grown on-site from seed, a practice that allows them to offer rare and unusual plants you can't find at a typical garden center or nursery. Arcana has the largest, most diverse, certified organic herbaceous perennial selection in Vermont. They also sell a wide variety of annual flowers, herbs, and vegetable seedlings, as well as growing produce for their mail-order website (arcanagardens.com) and farmers' market customers. See page 30 for their recipe for Celeriac, Fennel, and Leek Chowder Baked in Winter Squash, pictured here.

Celeriac, Fennel, and Leek Chowder Baked in Winter Squash

SERVES 8

When roasted, the soft, slightly sweet squash "meat" is delicious scooped into the chowder for additional flavor and texture. The reserved fennel fronds make a beautiful, edible garnish for this dish. See photo on page 29.

4 tablespoons (2 ounces) unsalted butter

2 leeks, white part only, halved lengthwise, cleaned and julienned

1 fennel bulb, fronds removed, chopped, and reserved; bulb quartered and julienned

4 cups vegetable stock, plus extra as needed

¼ cup light cream

1 teaspoon chopped fresh thyme

¼ teaspoon liquid smoke

Kosher salt and freshly ground black pepper

1 celeriac root (about 1 pound) peeled and diced

4 (2- to 3-pound) kabocha squash, cut in half horizontally

1. Preheat the oven to 350°F. Line a baking sheet with aluminum foil and set aside.

2. Heat 3 tablespoons of the butter in a large stockpot over medium heat. Add the leeks and fennel and sauté until the leeks are translucent and tender, about 8 minutes. Whisk in the stock and bring to a boil. Reduce the heat to medium-low and simmer for 10 minutes. Remove from the heat and let cool slightly. Working in batches, purée half of the soup in a blender or food processor until smooth. Return the purée to the stockpot with the remaining soup and stir in the cream, thyme, and liquid smoke. Season with salt and pepper to taste. If the soup is too thick, thin with additional vegetable stock.

3. Meanwhile, heat the remaining tablespoon of butter in a medium skillet over medium heat. Add the celeriac and sauté, stirring often, until light golden brown, about 8 minutes.

4. Scrape the seeds and pulp from the squash halves with a melon baller or spoon. (Reserve the seeds for toasting, if desired.) Sprinkle the inside of each squash bowl with salt and pepper and arrange them on the prepared baking sheet. Divide the celeriac among the squash bowls, and ladle the soup evenly into each bowl. Bake until the squash is tender when tested with a fork, 60 to 65 minutes. Garnish with the reserved chopped fennel fronds and serve.

Arcana Gardens and Greenhouses

ROASTED SQUASH SEEDS

Pumpkins are not the only winter squash that have great seeds for roasting. Acorn, kabocha, and butternut squash seeds are just as delicious roasted. You can eat the roasted seeds by themselves as a healthy snack or use them in salads, soups, and risotto dishes.

Preheat the oven to 325°F. Rinse the squash seeds to remove any pulp and drain them well. Place them in a large bowl and toss with just enough olive oil to coat. Spread the seeds in an even layer on an ungreased baking sheet and season with fine sea salt to taste. Bake, stirring occasionally, until the seeds are dry and lightly golden brown, about 20 minutes. Let cool. The seeds can be stored in an airtight container at room temperature.

Vermont Cheddar Soup

SERVES 6 AS A FIRST COURSE

One of the all-time favorite recipes at Simon Pearce, this creamy soup, created by former Simon Pearce chef Paul Langhans, is deliciously addictive. The soup is best the day after it is made; the flavors develop over time. It has a creamy, velvet-like texture with a slight acidic bite from the cheddar cheese. Be sure to use your favorite Vermont-made extra-sharp cheddar cheese. Serve alongside Rory's Irish Scones (page 16) and enjoy two of Simon Pearce's most popular flavors.

½ cup grated carrots

½ cup minced celery

8 tablespoons (4 ounces) unsalted butter

1 small onion, finely chopped

1 teaspoon chopped fresh thyme

1 bay leaf

½ cup all-purpose flour

4 cups chicken or vegetable stock, hot

12 ounces extra-sharp Vermont cheddar cheese, shredded (3 cups)

1 cup half-and-half, plus extra as needed

Kosher salt and freshly ground pepper

Chopped fresh parsley

Worcestershire sauce

1. Bring a medium saucepan of water to a boil, add the carrots and celery, and cook for 30 seconds. Drain well and set aside.

2. Melt the butter in a large saucepan over low heat. Add the onion, thyme, and bay leaf, increase the heat to medium-high, and cook until the onion is translucent.

3. Reduce the heat to low, add the flour, and cook, stirring, for 2 minutes. Turn the heat to medium-high and cook until the roux bubbles. Add the stock 1 cup at a time, making sure the liquid is at a boil the entire time, and whisk until smooth.

4. Add the cheddar cheese to the soup in two batches and stir until the cheese has melted. Add the half-and-half, carrots, and celery; if necessary, add extra half-and-half to thin the soup to the desired consistency. Remove the bay leaves and season with salt and pepper to taste. Garnish with parsley and a drizzle of Worcestershire sauce, if desired, and serve.

Simon Pearce

Tomato Coconut Soup

SERVES 4

Cedar Circle Farm served this soup garnished with purple basil, fresh coconut cream, and lime sugar at their 2011 Tomato Tasting. It was a huge hit! The success of the soup depends upon the quality of the ingredients. Use ripe, flavorful tomatoes to make the paste, good quality coconut milk that doesn't contain any guar gum or preservatives and homemade chicken stock—ideally from pastured or certified organic poultry. This soup is best served barely warmed on a hot summer's day, with crusty bread or a salad.

2 tablespoons extra-virgin olive oil

1 large sweet onion, finely chopped

1½ cups Homemade Tomato Paste (recipe follows)

2–2½ cups chicken stock

1½ cups coconut milk

Salt and freshly ground pepper

4 fresh basil leaves, thinly sliced

Fresh lime juice

Lime Sugar (recipe follows)

1. Heat the oil in a large saucepan over low heat. Add the onion and cook, stirring occasionally, until soft and just faintly colored, 15 to 20 minutes. Increase the heat to medium, add the tomato paste and stir, browning the tomato paste. Add 2 cups of the stock and the coconut milk and bring the soup just to a boil. Lower the heat and simmer gently for 5 minutes to allow the flavors to merge.

2. Working in batches, transfer the soup to a blender and purée until smooth. Return it to the pot and season with salt and pepper to taste. If the soup is too thick, add more chicken stock as needed. Serve warm with fresh basil, a splash of lime juice, and a sprinkle of lime sugar, if desired.

Alison Baker for Cedar Circle Farm

HOMEMADE TOMATO PASTE

MAKES ABOUT 1½ CUPS

6 pounds plum tomatoes (about 36 tomatoes)
Olive oil
Salt

1. Preheat the oven to 200°F. Line two large baking sheets with parchment paper.

2. Score each tomato by cutting an "X" on the underside. Set aside. Bring just enough water to cover the tomatoes to a boil in a large pot. Fill a large bowl halfway with ice water. Working in batches if necessary, with a slotted spoon, carefully place the tomatoes in the boiling water and blanch until the skins begin to crack, about 20 seconds. Carefully remove the tomatoes and place them in the ice water for 1 to 2 minutes. Remove the tomatoes from the water and peel off the skins.

3. Slice the tomatoes in half, remove the seeds, and place them on the prepared baking sheets cut side up. Sprinkle with oil and salt to taste, and bake until most of the liquid has evaporated and the tomatoes are sweet, 6 to 7 hours.

4. Let the tomatoes cool and then process them in a blender or food processor to make a light, loose tomato paste. Use immediately or freeze in an ice tray. Once frozen, pop them out and store in freezer-safe bags for later use.

LIME SUGAR

MAKES ABOUT 1½ CUPS

Remove the zest from 3 limes in strips with a vegetable peeler. Trim away any white pith from the zest (pith imparts a bitter flavor), and then chop the zest. Process the zest and 1 cup granulated sugar in a food processor until the mixture is pale green and bits of zest are still visible. Store in the refrigerator for up to 3 days.

Alison Baker for Cedar Circle Farm

Nettle Soup with Brioche Croutons

SERVES 6

When cleaning stinging nettles, wear rubber gloves to protect your hands. Remove and discard the woody stems and wash the leaves three times under cold running water.

4 tablespoons (2 ounces) unsalted butter

1 onion, minced

1 leek, white part only, finely diced

½ fennel bulb, minced

2 celery ribs, minced

1 shallot, minced

4 cups vegetable stock

8 ounces nettles, stemmed and cleaned

1 tablespoon sherry vinegar

Kosher salt and freshly ground pepper

1 ounce trout roe, plus more for garnish

1 teaspoon fresh lemon juice, or to taste

6 wood sorrel sprigs

Brioche Croutons (recipe follows)

1. In a large stockpot, melt 2 tablespoons of the butter over medium heat. Add the onion, leek, fennel, celery, and shallot and sauté, stirring occasionally, until the onion is soft and translucent, 6 to 7 minutes.

2. Add the vegetable stock and bring to a boil over medium-high heat. Add the nettles and cook until soft and tender, about 2 minutes. Working in batches, purée the soup in a blender or food processor until smooth. Return the soup to the pot and add the vinegar and 1 tablespoon butter. Bring to a simmer and continue cooking until heated through. Season with salt and pepper to taste.

3. Place the remaining 1 tablespoon butter in small skillet over medium heat and cook until light brown. Add the trout roe and lemon juice and cook until heated through.

4. Ladle the soup into bowls and garnish with the trout roe, sorrel sprigs, and croutons. Serve.

Misery Loves Co.

BRIOCHE CROUTONS

1 (12-ounce) loaf Brioche (page 24) or challah bread, cut into ¾-inch cubes (6 to 8 cups)

2½ tablespoons extra-virgin olive oil or 3½ tablespoons unsalted butter, melted

Kosher salt and freshly ground black pepper

Preheat the oven to 350°F. In a large bowl, toss the bread cubes with the olive oil and season with salt and pepper to taste. Spread the bread out in a single layer on a baking sheet and bake, tossing occasionally, until golden brown, 10 to 15 minutes. Let cool to room temperature. Store in an airtight container.

Misery Loves Co.

HIGH RIDGE MEADOWS FARM

High Ridge Meadows Farm is a small family-run, organically managed farm located in the hills of East Randolph. The goal of the owners, Mary and Jim Moran, is to raise the best grass-fed beef, lamb, and poultry possible, as well as premium livestock and wool. All of the farm's animals are raised using organic standards and are given ample pasture to graze and pure spring water to drink. Eggs, meat, maple syrup, and woolen products are sold through their farm store and online. The farm also operates a wedding and events venue, The Barn on the Hill.

The Morans are thrilled to be farming in Vermont, and they enjoy all the state has to offer. They feel it's important to preserve the beautiful mix of mountains, forests, and fields that are so unique to this state, and they're honored to continue its history of farming.

Musquée de Provence Pumpkin Bisque

MAKES 12 CUPS

Musquée de Provence is a French heirloom pumpkin variety, also known as the Fairytale Pumpkin. It is large and deeply ridged, with sweet flesh. You could substitute Hubbard squash or a sweet pie pumpkin. You will need 5 to 6 pounds of pumpkin for the purée. If possible, use organic coconut milk in this recipe.

1 tablespoon unsalted butter

1 large yellow onion, chopped

4 large garlic cloves, chopped

4 cups low-sodium chicken broth

3¼ cups fresh Musquée de Provence pumpkin purée (recipe follows), or 2 (15-ounce) cans pumpkin purée

2 large Granny Smith apples, peeled, cored, and chopped

1 jalapeño pepper, stemmed, seeded, and finely chopped

2 tablespoons pure Vermont maple syrup

2 teaspoons ground coriander

½ teaspoon ground cumin

Kosher salt and freshly ground black pepper

1 (14-ounce) can unsweetened coconut milk

Chopped fresh thyme (optional)

1. Melt the butter in a large stockpot over medium heat. Add the onion and cook, stirring occasionally, until soft and translucent, about 5 minutes. Add the garlic, stirring frequently, and cook for 1 minute.

2. Add the broth, pumpkin purée, apples, jalapeño, maple syrup, coriander, cumin, and 1½ teaspoons salt and bring to a boil over medium-high heat. Reduce the heat to a simmer and cook, stirring occasionally, for 30 minutes. Let cool for 10 minutes.

3. Working in batches, purée the soup in a blender or food processor, adding the coconut milk a little bit at a time, until smooth. Return the soup to the stockpot and cook until heated through. Season with salt and pepper to taste. Ladle the soup into cups and garnish with thyme, if desired.

High Ridge Meadows Farm

FRESH PUMPKIN PURÉE

Preheat the oven to 375°F. Halve a 5- to 6-pound Musquée de Provence pumpkin and remove the seeds and strings. Rub the inside of the pumpkin with 1 tablespoon butter. Place, skin side down, in a large roasting pan and add enough water to generously cover the bottom of the pan. Roast until the flesh is fork-tender, about 45 minutes. Remove from the oven and let cool. When cool enough to handle, remove and discard the skin. Place the pumpkin meat in a blender or food processor, and purée until smooth.

MT. MANSFIELD CREAMERY

Mt. Mansfield Creamery produces handcrafted, small-batch cheeses of European origins. The family milks a mixed herd of grass-fed Holstein and Brown Swiss cows. The cheeses are named after famous ski trails at Stowe, where cheesemaker Stan Biasini is a part-time ski and ride instructor in the winter season.

Creamy Camembert Cheese and Potato Soup with Black Pepper Croutons

SERVES 8 TO 10

This creamy, rich soup is not only delicious but also easy to make. Keith Smith, a student from the New England Culinary Institute, created the soup using only local ingredients, which he found at the Capital City Farmers' Market. Looking for inspiration, Keith walked through the market gathering ideas and ingredients. He then prepared the soup right at the market and handed out samples for folks to try. It was a big hit! All-purpose potatoes are moderately starchy white potatoes.

Croutons

½ **baguette, cubed**

¼ **cup olive oil**

Kosher salt and freshly ground black pepper

Soup

3 **tablespoons unsalted butter**

2 **sweet onions, such as Vidalia or Walla Walla, thinly sliced**

1 **small garlic clove, minced**

⅛ **teaspoon celery salt**

3 **medium all-purpose potatoes, peeled and cut into 1-inch chunks**

2½ **cups vegetable stock, plus extra as needed**

1 **cup milk**

½ **cup heavy cream**

5 **ounces Camembert cheese, cut into small pieces**

¼ **teaspoon chopped fresh thyme or sage**

Salt and freshly ground white pepper

1. To make the croutons: Preheat the oven to 350°F. Toss the bread cubes with the oil, salt, and pepper to taste. Transfer to a baking sheet and toast, tossing occasionally, until golden brown for about 15 minutes. Let cool.

2. To make the soup: Melt the butter in a large, heavy saucepan over medium-high heat. Add the onions, garlic, and celery salt and cook until the onions are soft but not brown. Add the potatoes, stirring to coat with butter, and cook for 5 minutes.

3. Add the stock and bring to a boil. Reduce the heat to medium-low, cover, and simmer until the potatoes are fork-tender, about 30 minutes. Let the soup cool slightly, then whisk in the milk and cream in a slow, steady stream. Reheat the soup over low heat. Stir in the cheese until melted.

4. Transfer the soup to a blender and purée in batches until smooth. Return soup to the saucepan and add the thyme and season with salt and pepper to taste. Thin with additional stock if necessary. Serve immediately, garnished with croutons, or refrigerate and serve cold.

Note: The croutons can be made ahead and stored in an airtight container for up to two days.

Mt. Mansfield Creamery and the
Capital City Farmers' Market

Ski Vermont Farmhouse Potato Chowder

SERVES 4 TO 6

Sugarbush Resort is a four-season resort located in the heart of Vermont, in the farm-rich Mad River Valley. The culinary team at Sugarbush takes full advantage of the produce, cheese, and livestock that thrive in the surrounding area. With several restaurants and a spectacular natural setting, Sugarbush offers an array of locally inspired dining choices that appeal to almost any palate. The resort's former executive chef, Gerry Nooney, was named Vermont Chef of the Year in 2009, thanks, in part, to his commitment to cooking with local foods. When the Vermont Department of Agriculture asked Nooney to assist them in finding a way to help Vermont farmers sell more potatoes, he created this hearty chowder. It was inspired by both New England clam chowder and traditional leek and potato soup.

1¼ pounds potatoes, peeled and diced

4 cups chicken stock

¾ cup Vermont apple cider

1 (4-ounce) link hot Italian sausage

2 tablespoons vegetable oil

1 small Spanish onion, diced

1 large celery rib, finely chopped

1 teaspoon smoked paprika

½ cup heavy cream

2 teaspoons chopped fresh marjoram

2 teaspoons chopped fresh basil

Kosher salt and freshly ground black pepper

continues . . .

1. Place 12 ounces of the potatoes in a large stockpot and cover with the chicken stock and cider. Bring to a simmer over medium-high heat and cook until the potatoes are very tender, about 10 minutes. Transfer potatoes and liquid to a blender and purée until smooth. Return the soup to the stockpot.

2. Meanwhile, place the sausage in a small skillet, add 1 cup water, and bring to a simmer over medium heat. Cook, turning the sausage occasionally, until the sausage is plump. Let the sausage cool, then coarsely chop and add to the soup.

3. Discard the water from the skillet, wipe it clean, and place over medium heat. Add the oil, onion, and celery and cook, stirring frequently, until the onion is translucent. Add the paprika and cook 3 minutes, stirring often. Add the vegetables to the soup. Slowly stir in the cream.

4. Meanwhile, place the remaining 8 ounces of potatoes in a medium saucepan, cover with salted water, and bring to a simmer over medium-high heat. Cook the potatoes until fork-tender, about 10 minutes. Drain and rinse under cold water. Add to the soup mixture and return the soup to a simmer. Add the marjoram and basil and season with salt and pepper to taste. Serve.

Sugarbush Resort/Rumble's Bistro & Bar

JOE'S KITCHEN AT SCREAMIN' RIDGE FARM

Joe Buley's grandmother's kitchen is the inspiration for the products he creates at his business, Joe's Kitchen at Screamin' Ridge Farm. When cooking, his grandmother used whatever she had on hand, supplemented by her ample supply of spices. His mom continued the tradition, spending many hours in the kitchen cooking with him.

Building a career as a restaurant chef and entrepreneur, Joe trained in France at L'École Supérieure de Cuisine Française. There he learned the importance of starting with fresh, high-quality ingredients. After returning to the United States, he moved his family to East Montpelier, Vermont, in 1999. There, he bought a house with 7.5 acres of land and began to learn how to farm. During the time he was getting the farm up and running, he also worked as a chef-instructor at the New England Culinary Institute.

Screamin' Ridge Farm slowly grew into a successful business. Connecting with customers through farmers' markets and his farm's CSA, Joe saw that there was both a need and a demand for preparing healthy meals from raw farm products. He realized that this was the time to pursue his vision of culinary-supported agriculture by growing ingredients and using them to cook deliciously prepared meals.

Joe is not interested in high volume production; his emphasis is on the best quality possible. He began his enterprise with mouthwatering hot soups, which were made available at the Montpelier Farmers' Market. Most of the produce and herbs that are used are grown on Joe's small farm. If the need should arise, additional produce, meat, and cheese are purchased from local producers. The emphasis is on creating delicious, healthy food by using local ingredients that are sustainably grown whenever possible. Joe Buley wants consumers to know that supporting and buying local helps to preserve Vermont's working landscape.

All of Screamin' Ridge Farm's yield is used by their commercial kitchen in Montpelier. The recipes are created by Joe, using simple and clean ingredients. When asked about his favorite dish, Joe acknowledges that many happy memories are associated with his myriad of soups. He even makes his own stocks. It is not surprising that split pea soup is one of his favorites; it reminds him of his mother.

Lemon Ginger Roast Chicken with Brown Rice Soup

SERVES 6 TO 8

The inspiration for Buley's soups comes from his grandmother's kitchen in East Randolph. With equal regard for flavor and economy, his grandmother used whatever was on hand—from leftover roasted chicken to potatoes, onions, and vegetables picked from the garden, all of which were pulled together to create a great-tasting soup. This is a time- and labor-intensive soup to make, but well worth the effort. It offers an Asian twist on traditional chicken and rice soup.

1 (5-pound) whole chicken, preferably free-range, giblets removed

2 tablespoons olive oil

Kosher salt and freshly ground black pepper

4 ounces short- or medium-grain brown rice, rinsed

8 ounces onions, chopped

8 ounces carrots, chopped

8 ounces celery, chopped

2 cups dry white wine

Grated zest and juice from 3 lemons

2 tablespoons grated fresh ginger

2 garlic cloves, minced

1 teaspoon red pepper flakes

⅓ cup minced fresh parsley

Rice wine vinegar (optional)

1. Preheat the oven to 375°F. Rinse the chicken and pat dry with paper towels. Rub with 1 tablespoon oil and season generously inside and out with salt and pepper. Place breast side up in a roasting pan. Roast the chicken, basting every 15 minutes, until the skin is golden brown, juices run clear, and the chicken reaches an internal temperature of 160°F, about 1¼ hours.

2. When the chicken is cool enough to handle, remove the skin and set aside for the stock. Using two forks or your fingertips, shred or pull the meat from the bones and set aside.

3. Place the chicken carcass, skin, and 8 cups water in a stockpot. Bring to a boil over medium-high heat. Reduce the heat and simmer for 30 minutes. Strain the stock through a fine-mesh strainer into a medium bowl.

4. Place 1 gallon of water in a pot and bring to a boil over medium-high heat. Add the rice, cover tightly, and cook until tender, about 15 minutes. Strain and set aside.

5. Heat the remaining 1 tablespoon oil in a stockpot over medium heat. Add the onions, carrots, and celery and cook, stirring occasionally, until the onions are soft and translucent, about 10 minutes. Stir in the reserved chicken stock.

6. Purée the wine, lemon zest and juice, ginger, garlic, and red pepper flakes in a blender or food processor until smooth. Add to the stockpot with vegetables and bring to a boil over medium-high heat. Reduce the heat to a simmer, add the chicken, brown rice, and parsley, and continue cooking until heated through. Season with salt and pepper to taste; if the soup is too thick, add water as needed. Ladle into soup bowls, drizzle with rice wine vinegar, if desired, and serve.

Joe's Kitchen at Screamin' Ridge Farm

STERLING COLLEGE

Sterling is a progressive liberal arts college located in the heart of Vermont's Northeast Kingdom. Sterling is distinguished by its small size, ecological focus, commitment to grassroots sustainability, and year-round schedule. The college is the only federally designated Work College in New England, offers continuing education, operates three instructional farms, and offers the tuition-free Wendell Berry Farming Program. The dining hall at Sterling practices a live-what-you-teach philosophy, focusing on food that is sustainable, local, delicious, and nutritions. Over the course of a year, Sterling undergraduate students grow about 30 percent of the food saved in the dining hall. A total of 84 percent of food served is produced locally or regionally. The school's cooking focuses on creative and delicious ways of using everything that is abundant in their part of the world, be it beets, cabbage, lamb, or cheese.

Roasted Beet Salad with Cilantro and Lime

SERVES 6

From late spring through the winter, some version of this beet salad is almost a constant in the Sterling dining hall. It's a great dish for non-beet lovers because the citrus juice, or vinegar, tempers the earthy taste of this root. Don't dry the beets after scrubbing them; the moisture helps them cook.

8 medium red beets, tops removed, scrubbed

1 teaspoon cumin seeds

½ cup chopped fresh cilantro

4 scallions, thinly sliced

**½ cup fresh lime or lemon juice
   (from 4 limes or 3 lemons)**

2 tablespoons extra-virgin olive oil

Kosher salt and freshly ground black pepper

1. Preheat the oven to 400°F.

2. Place a large sheet of aluminum foil on a baking sheet. Put the beets (still wet from being scrubbed) in the center and carefully wrap them in the foil, making an airtight packet. Roast until fork-tender, 1 to 1¼ hours. Set aside to cool.

3. Toast the cumin seeds in a small nonstick skillet over medium-high heat, stirring frequently, until the seeds are dry and fragrant, about 30 seconds. Crush the seeds with a mortar and pestle, or on a cutting board with the bottom of a frying pan. Set aside.

4. When the beets are cool enough to handle, use a paper towel to gently rub off their skins. Chop the beets into wedges and place in a large bowl. Add the cilantro, scallions, citrus juice, oil, cumin, and salt and pepper to taste. Toss to coat and set aside to marinate for 30 minutes. Serve.

Note: The salad will keep, refrigerated, for up to 3 days.

Sterling College

Late Summer Quinoa Salad

MAKES 4 CUPS

Quinoa is a versatile whole grain that was once a staple of the ancient Incas. Unlike other grains, quinoa contains a good balance of the nine essential amino acids, making it a complete protein. It cooks quickly, and doesn't have as strong a flavor as other whole grains. It's about the same size as couscous, and is a great choice when you want more fiber, protein, and nutrients without the extra time or work.

Feel free to substitute other vegetables and flavorings for the ones in this recipe. Quinoa salad is great with roasted butternut squash cubes and walnuts instead of tomatoes and corn. In the winter, try sun-dried tomatoes and black olives with red wine vinegar instead of apple cider vinegar. Quinoa is a great backdrop to highlight whatever is local and in season. This salad is best eaten the day it's made.

1 cup quinoa, rinsed and drained

2 cups water

3 tablespoons extra-virgin olive oil

4 ears corn, kernels cut from cobs

1 cup cherry tomatoes cut into quarters

4 scallions, thinly sliced

½ cup chopped fresh parsley

½ cup Vermont apple cider vinegar

Kosher salt and freshly ground black pepper

1. Combine the quinoa and water in a small saucepan and bring to a boil over high heat. Cover, reduce the heat, and simmer until the quinoa is tender and the water is absorbed, 10 to 15 minutes. Let cool.

2. Heat 2 tablespoons of the oil in a medium cast-iron skillet over medium-high heat until very hot. Add the corn kernels and cook, stirring constantly, until slightly blackened on the outside and barely cooked inside, about 30 seconds. Spread the corn kernels out on a plate in a single layer to cool.

3. Transfer the corn to a large bowl and add the quinoa, tomatoes, scallions, and parsley. Stir in the vinegar and remaining 1 tablespoon oil and season with salt and pepper to taste. Set aside to marinate at least 30 minutes or up to 3 hours. Serve.

Variations: This salad is delicious with other types of vinegars such as sherry, champagne, red wine, or apple cider. Try it with diced sweet white onions, scallions, or garlic. You can also add different herbs, such as chopped mint or dill.

Sterling College

CLEAR BROOK FARM

Andrew Knafel started Clear Brook Farm in 1994. The farm is located along historic Route 7A in Shaftsbury, Vermont. With the help of an amazing crew of dedicated farmers who work alongside Andrew, Clear Brook has grown from producing organic vegetables on one acre with one greenhouse, to growing 30 acres of organic crops every year. There are also many greenhouses that produce "starts" for home gardeners, as well as organic vegetables that are grown long into Vermont's winter months.

Plants and produce can be purchased from Clear Brook's farm stand, which is open during the months of May through October. Knafel also offers a summer farm stand CSA, an autumn CSA that goes from mid-October to Christmas, and a "Deep Winter" CSA in January and February.

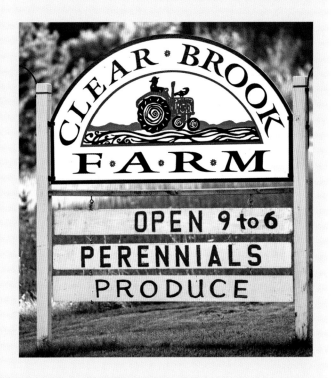

Arugula, Fig, and Goat Cheese Salad with Orange Vinaigrette

SERVES 4

The orange vinaigrette is light, with subtle citrus undertones, which allow all the layers of flavor in the salad to emerge.

3 tablespoons fresh orange juice

1½ tablespoons white wine vinegar or Vermont apple cider vinegar

1 teaspoon sherry

¼ cup extra-virgin olive oil, plus extra for the goat cheese

Kosher salt and freshly ground black pepper

4-ounce fresh goat cheese log, cut into 4 disks

2 bunches arugula, torn into bite-sized pieces

8 fresh ripe black Mission figs, quartered

½ cup toasted walnuts, chopped

1. Preheat the oven to 375°F. Spray a baking sheet with nonstick cooking spray.

2. In a small bowl, whisk together the orange juice, vinegar, sherry, and oil. Season with salt and pepper to taste. Brush the goat cheese rounds with oil and place on the prepared baking sheet. Bake until just warmed through, about 5 minutes.

3. Combine the arugula, figs, and walnuts in a large bowl. Add the vinaigrette and toss to combine. Divide the salad among four plates and place one cheese round in the center of each salad; serve.

Clear Brook Farm

PEBBLE BROOK FARM

Pebble Brook Farm is a small certified organic farm located in Braintree. The farm, owned and operated by Chip and Sarah Natvig, is known for its salad greens and heirloom tomatoes. They grow a variety of produce and storage crops, which they sell through a small member CSA, as well as at their farm store on location.

Turnip Greens and Red Leaf Lettuce with Onion, Corn, and Basil Vinaigrette

SERVES 4 TO 6

This salad is all about textures and depth of favor. Each component contributes something different, from the crisp turnip greens and crunchy croutons to the soft, sweet onion and starchy, caramelized corn. The earthy aroma of the basil pesto collaborates with the fresh lemon to give a punch of brightness.

Vinaigrette

⅓ cup chopped fresh basil

⅓ cup fresh lemon juice (2 to 3 lemons)

2 tablespoons shaved Parmesan cheese

1 teaspoon whole-grain mustard

1 garlic clove, minced

Pinch red pepper flakes

2 tablespoons extra-virgin olive oil

2 tablespoons vegetable oil

Kosher salt and freshly ground black pepper

Croutons and Salad

12 ounces baguette, cut into 1-inch cubes (about 3 cups)

½ cup extra-virgin olive oil

Kosher salt and freshly ground black pepper

1 medium red or sweet onion, thinly sliced

2 ears corn, kernels cut from cobs

3 garlic cloves, minced

1 bunch baby turnip greens, torn into bite-sized pieces

1 head red leaf lettuce, torn into bite-sized pieces

1. Preheat the oven to 350°F.

2. To make the vinaigrette: In a small bowl whisk together the basil, lemon juice, Parmesan, mustard, garlic, and pepper flakes. Whisking vigorously, add the olive oil and vegetable oil in a slow, steady stream. Season with salt and pepper to taste and set aside.

3. To make the croutons and salad: In a medium bowl, toss the bread cubes with ¼ cup oil and salt and pepper to taste. Transfer to a baking sheet and toast, tossing occasionally, until golden brown, about 15 minutes. Remove from the oven and let cool. Increase the oven temperature to 400°F.

4. Place the onion slices on a baking sheet and toss with 1 tablespoon olive oil. Roast for 20 to 25 minutes and set aside.

5. While the onion is roasting, heat 1 tablespoon olive oil in a medium skillet over medium-high heat. Add the corn kernels and cook until light golden brown, 8 to 10 minutes. Remove from the heat and set aside.

6. Heat the remaining 2 tablespoons oil over in a small saucepan over medium heat. Add the garlic and cook until fragrant but not browned, 2 to 3 minutes. Let the oil cool, then combine with the corn.

7. In a large bowl, combine the turnip greens and red leaf lettuce and toss with the vinaigrette to taste. Top with the onion, corn, and croutons and serve.

Pebble Brook Farm

CITY MARKET, ONION RIVER CO-OP

City Market, Onion River Co-op, is a community-owned food cooperative with two locations in beautiful Burlington, Vermont. With over 12,000 members, the Co-op offers a large selection of local, organic, and conventional foods, and thousands of Vermont-made products. City Market is committed to strengthening the local food system and increasing food access in the greater Burlington area.

Massaged Kale Salad with Asian Peanut Dressing

SERVES 4

All of the massaged kale salad recipes that Meg Klepack, the former outreach and local food manager of City Market, found used a simple olive oil and sea salt dressing. Bored with olive oil–coated kale, Klepack had an epiphany—she could use any of the more interesting dressings that were made for green salads for the massaged kale salad. She adapted an Asian-style peanut dressing from another recipe, and the result was pure kale bliss. If peaches are not in season, you can easily substitute apples in this salad. Feel free to use walnuts or sunflower seeds in place of pepitas. The flavor of the kale mellows as you massage it with the dressing; you can add more dressing to suit your taste.

⅓ cup pepitas

1 teaspoon extra-virgin olive oil

¼ teaspoon kosher salt

1 bunch curly green kale, stemmed and cut into bite-sized pieces

½ cup Asian Peanut Dressing (recipe follows), plus extra to taste

2 small peaches, pitted and diced

2 ounces feta cheese, crumbled (½ cup)

1. Place the pepitas, oil, and salt in a medium skillet and toss to coat. Toast over medium heat until the pepitas turn light brown and start to pop, 2 to 3 minutes. Remove from the pan and set aside on paper towels.

2. In a large bowl, combine the kale and half of the dressing. Using your hands or tongs, massage the kale until it is bright green and slightly softened, 2 to 3 minutes, adding more dressing to taste. Top with the pepitas, peaches, and feta. Serve at once.

City Market, Onion River Co-op

ASIAN PEANUT DRESSING

MAKES 1⅓ CUPS

This dressing can be stored in the refrigerator for up to one month.

¼ cup rice vinegar

¼ cup soy sauce

3 tablespoons plain yogurt

4 teaspoons grated ginger

4 teaspoons sesame oil

4 garlic cloves, minced

1 tablespoon peanut butter

2 teaspoons chili garlic sauce

1½ teaspoons brown sugar

Whisk together all the ingredients until combined.

MANCHESTER FARMERS' MARKET

Since 2001, the Manchester Farmers' Market has provided consumers with an array of farm-fresh produce, cheeses, eggs, and meats, locally prepared foods, as well as quality crafts and artisan wares. The outside marketplace also offers live music every week—free of charge.

Patriotic Potato Salad

SERVES 6 TO 8

Try to buy small potatoes of a uniform size so they will cook at the same rate. Good varieties to try include Red Rosa, German Butterball, and Adirondack Blue. Vary the amount of dill, basil, and celery salt to suit your taste.

1 pound small red-skinned potatoes

1 pound small white-skinned, waxy-style potatoes

1 pound small purple or blue potatoes

4 slices thick-cut bacon

Salt and freshly ground black pepper

1 cup Simple Mayonnaise, plus extra as needed (recipe follows)

1 cup chopped celery

1 small onion, finely chopped

1 tablespoon Vermont apple cider vinegar

1 tablespoon Dijon mustard

1 tablespoon fresh chopped dill

1 tablespoon fresh chopped basil

⅛ teaspoon celery salt

3 large hard-boiled eggs, peeled and chopped

1. Combine the potatoes and ½ teaspoon salt in a large pot, cover with water, and boil over medium-high heat. Reduce heat and cook until fork-tender, 10 to 15 minutes. Drain the potatoes in a colander and set aside to cool. When cool enough to handle, cut into ½-inch-thick slices.

2. While the potatoes simmer, cook the bacon in a medium skillet over medium-high heat until crisp, 5 to 7 minutes. Drain on paper towels, then crumble.

3. Stir together the mayonnaise, celery, onion, vinegar, mustard, dill, basil, and celery salt in a bowl large enough to hold the potatoes. Fold in the potatoes and eggs and season with salt and pepper to taste. Sprinkle with the crumbled bacon and serve.

SIMPLE MAYONNAISE

MAKES 1 CUP

1 large egg yolk

1–2 tablespoons fresh lemon juice

½ teaspoon freshly ground black pepper

¼ teaspoon kosher salt

¾ cup canola or safflower oil, plus extra as needed

Process the egg yolk, 1 tablespoon lemon juice, pepper, and salt in a food processor to combine. With the motor running, slowly add the oil in a steady stream until well blended and the mixture has thickened; if necessary, add more oil until desired consistency has been achieved. Transfer to a bowl and add lemon juice to taste. Use immediately or cover and refrigerate for up to 2 days.

Note: When using raw eggs, use only high-quality, in-shell pasteurized eggs that are clean and have been properly refrigerated.

Manchester Farmers' Market

EARTH SKY TIME COMMUNITY FARM

Earth Sky Time Community Farm, located in Manchester, is a small community-based, year-round certified organic farm. The farm not only grows vegetables, orchard fruit, herbs, and flowers on approximately 10 acres of land, but also runs a commercial kitchen and wood-fired bakery. All of their products are vegetarian, globally inspired, homemade prepared foods such as Vermont Goldburgers, hummus, and salsa. They bake a wide range of artisanal breads (mostly sourdough) in a Llopis oven, which is a wood-fired brick oven made in Spain. The owners, Oliver and Bonnie Levis, sell their produce and value-added products at their on-site farm stand, as well as at farmers' markets.

Red Cabbage and Carrot Slaw with Cilantro Vinaigrette

SERVES 6

This vibrant slaw uses cilantro-infused vinegar, which must steep for four days, so prepare accordingly.

Vinaigrette

½ cup fresh orange juice

½ cup Cilantro-Infused Vinegar (recipe follows)

2 tablespoons Vermont honey

1 tablespoon grated ginger

1 tablespoon fresh lime juice

3 tablespoons toasted sesame oil, plus extra to taste

Kosher salt and freshly ground black pepper

Cabbage and Carrot Slaw

4 cups finely shredded red cabbage (about ½ head)

2 cups shredded carrots (3 to 4 carrots)

2–3 tablespoons toasted sesame seeds

1. To make the vinaigrette: Whisk together the orange juice, vinegar, honey, ginger, and lime juice in a small bowl. Slowly whisk in the oil until well combined. Season with salt and pepper to taste.

2. To make the cabbage and carrot slaw: Combine the cabbage and carrots in a large bowl. Drizzle with the vinaigrette and toss to coat. Season with salt and pepper to taste. Cover and refrigerate for 2 to 3 hours before serving. Garnish with toasted sesame seeds, if desired.

CILANTRO-INFUSED VINEGAR

1½ cups fresh cilantro leaves, lightly crushed

1 cup Vermont apple cider vinegar

Place the cilantro in a 16-ounce glass jar with a tight lid. Add the vinegar and seal. Let sit at room temperature for 4 to 5 days. Strain the vinegar through a fine-mesh strainer into a clean jar. Cover and refrigerate for up to 2 weeks.

Earth Sky Time Community Farm

WOODSTOCK FARMERS' MARKET

The Woodstock Farmers' Market is a year-round mecca of fantastic food with two locations in Woodstock and Waterbury, Vermont. The market offers wholesome foods that include fresh organic produce, local meats, specialty and everyday grocery products, coffee and espresso, baked goods, prepared foods, and more.

"Celebrating more than 30 years (1992–2023) as the preeminent specialty food store in Vermont, our communities in Woodstock and Waterbury have relied on our kitchens to inspire creativity in the kitchen, feed families, and celebrate occasions. More importantly, when it comes to cooking at home, we believe anyone can create great food—but you need great regional and local ingredients to elevate your flavor profiles. And we are fortunate to have a long list of amazing farmers and producers, supplying us with fresh and delicious meal ingredients right here in Vermont.

Today, more than ever, knowing where your food comes from is paramount. Our staff takes the job of 'bringing the food to the people' seriously. We curate food and ingredients and keep solid relationships with great producers and farmers from all over New England. Our customers appreciate that connection and feel that supporting their local food network is one of the most important things they can do for themselves and for their community."

Bow Thai Pasta Salad

SERVES 6 TO 8

In 1992, Amelia Rappaport, a New England Culinary Institute graduate, was hired to start the prepared foods department for the Woodstock Farmers' Market. She made Bow Thai Pasta Salad occasionally, in rotation with other pasta salads. Today, Amelia is a part owner in the business and Bow Thai Pasta Salad is made daily by popular demand. This recipe makes more dressing than you will need for the pasta. It will keep, refrigerated, for up to three weeks and can be used as salad dressing or marinade.

Salt
1 pound farfalle
⅔ cup canola oil
½ cup soy sauce
½ cup rice vinegar
⅓ cup chili oil
2 tablespoons sesame oil
2 large garlic cloves, finely minced
¼ teaspoon cayenne pepper
1½ cups creamy peanut butter
½ cup chopped red bell pepper
½ cup thinly sliced scallions
¼ cup sesame seeds, toasted

1. Bring a large pot of salted water to a boil. Add the pasta and cook until al dente, about 8 minutes. Drain the pasta, transfer to a large bowl, and let cool.

2. In a medium bowl, whisk together the canola oil, soy sauce, vinegar, chili oil, sesame oil, garlic, and cayenne. Whisk in the peanut butter until smooth.

3. Add 1 cup of the dressing to the pasta and stir to coat; add more dressing as needed. Season with salt to taste, sprinkle with peppers, scallions, and sesame seeds, and serve.

Amelia Rappaport and the Woodstock Farmers' Market

Wheat Berry Salad with Fresh Herbs

SERVES 4 TO 6

Cedar Circle Farm served this salad at their ninth annual Strawberry Festival in June 2011 to show how delicious whole grains can be. More than a dozen people asked for the recipe that day—including a few kids! Wheat berries are the entire wheat kernel, minus the hull. The staff at Cedar Circle likes the heirloom wheat berries grown on the farm, but any organic variety will work. Chewy cooked wheat berries give this salad a lovely depth and a nutty flavor, and you can vary the vegetables and herbs according to the season and what's in your garden. Radishes and fresh mint are nice additions. If you don't have walnuts, pine nuts would be a good substitute. If you are unable to find a kohlrabi bulb, you can substitute ⅓ cup lightly steamed chopped broccoli stems and ¼ cup lightly steamed chopped golden turnip.

Vinaigrette

5 tablespoons brown rice vinegar, preferably organic

1 tablespoon fresh lime juice

1 tablespoon stone-ground mustard

1 teaspoon kosher salt

½ teaspoon freshly ground black pepper

6 tablespoons extra-virgin olive oil

Salad

1 cup hard wheat berries, preferably organic

2 celery ribs, diced

1 small kohlrabi bulb, peeled and diced

2 scallions, thinly sliced

¾ cup walnuts, toasted and chopped

½ cup dried cranberries (optional)

⅔ cup chopped fresh parsley

⅓ cup coarsely chopped basil (optional)

Kosher salt and freshly ground black pepper

1. To make the vinaigrette: Whisk together the vinegar, lime juice, mustard, salt, and pepper in a small bowl. Whisking vigorously, add the oil in a slow, steady stream.

2. To make the salad: Bring 2½ quarts salted water to a boil in a large saucepan. Add the wheat berries and cook uncovered, until tender, but still chewy, 1 to 1¼ hours.

3. Drain the wheat berries through a colander, then transfer to a large bowl. Add the vinaigrette and stir to coat. Stir in the celery, kohlrabi, scallions, walnuts, cranberries, if desired, and parsley and basil, if desired. Season with salt and pepper to taste. Serve warm or at room temperature.

Alison Baker for Cedar Circle Farm

Tyler Place Maple Balsamic Vinaigrette

MAKES ABOUT 3 CUPS

This is a very versatile dressing that is just as good as a marinade for chicken or pork tenderloin as it is drizzled over a bed of local mesclun greens. Make sure to use a high-quality balsamic vinegar in this dressing.

2 tablespoons coarsely chopped garlic

2 tablespoons coarsely chopped shallots

¼ cup balsamic vinegar

¼ cup pure Vermont maple syrup

1½ tablespoons Dijon mustard

1 teaspoon dried oregano

¼ teaspoon freshly ground black pepper

1 cup canola oil

1 cup extra-virgin olive oil

Hot water, as needed

Pulse the garlic and shallots in a food processor until they are minced. Add the vinegar, maple syrup, mustard, oregano, and pepper and pulse until well combined. While the machine is running, gradually add the oils until a creamy dressing forms. Season with salt and pepper to taste. If the dressing is too thick, add hot water, a little at a time, until the desired consistency is achieved.

The Tyler Place Family Resort

THE RELUCTANT PANTHER INN AND RESTAURANT

The Reluctant Panther Inn and Restaurant is southern Vermont's premier small luxury hotel. Located in the heart of historic Manchester Village, it has been in continual operation since the mid-1960s and offers 20 spacious, elegantly appointed rooms and suites and a top-rated gourmet dining experience. The Panther's restaurant specializes in contemporary American cuisine with an emphasis on locally sourced foods. Executive Chef Sigal Rocklin creates a sophisticated dining experience that is unsurpassed in northern New England.

The Reluctant Panther's name is a nod to the wild panthers that once roamed the nearby mountains despite the encroachment of humans. They symbolized the fierce, independent attitude of Vermonters, who fought against interference by the English king and from their neighbors to the east and west. At the Green Mountain Tavern, which stood on this site until 1897, Ethan Allen's Green Mountain boys met and organized their resistance. The name Reluctant Panther was conceived in the 1960; it pairs the reluctance of panthers to come down from the mountains with the historical symbolism of the property. The Reluctant Panther has been a Manchester institution ever since.

MAPLEBROOK FARM

In 2003, Michael Scheps, a third-generation cheesemaker, began producing hand-stretched mozzarella in the kitchen of Al Ducci's Italian Pantry, an Italian-style delicatessen and food market, in Manchester Center. Scheps was stretching out mozzarella cheese and putting the balls out on the counter for Al Ducci's customers when Johann Englert walked into the store. Immediately, she was drawn to the display of mozzarella balls. Englert hadn't seen mozzarella displayed in that fashion since a trip to Italy years before, so she decided to buy some. She immediately fell in love with the cheese and felt that it was the best mozzarella that she had tasted in the United States.

A natural entrepreneur, Englert approached Scheps with the idea of selling his cheese to Boston chefs. Initially, Englert took 20 mozzarella balls to Boston; five of the gourmet shops that sampled them ordered more, and before long, Scheps was scrambling to keep up with the orders Englert generated. The following year, the pair saw enough potential in their budding business to purchase a cheese plant in Bennington, Vermont, and launched what is now Maplebrook Farm.

Through the use of Old-World cheesemaking traditions, the company now handcrafts seven cheeses—handmade mozzarella, smoked mozzarella, hand-dipped ricotta, whole milk feta, burrata, cheddar bites, and mozzarella in water.

In 2022, Maplebrook partnered with Ploughgate Creamery and is producing Ploughgate's beautiful line of cultured butter and flavored butters in its now 40,000 square feet of production space in Bennington and North Bennington, Vermont. A new chapter in Maplebrook's story!

Maplebrook Farm's Burrata Salad with Local Spinach, Strawberries, Basil Pesto, Pistachios, and Aged Balsamic

SERVES 4; MAKES 1¾ CUPS OF PESTO

"Maplebrook Farm's burrata replicates old-world fashion by stretching curd into mozzarella and filling it with a luscious creamy center. The soft center, stracciatella, comprised of cream and stands of mozzarella gives this cheese a distinct flavor," shares Maplebrook Farm.

Basil Pesto

2 tightly packed cups fresh basil leaves

3 tablespoons raw pine nuts

½ cup grated Parmigiano-Reggiano cheese (about 2 ounces)

3 medium garlic cloves, coarsely chopped

½ teaspoon kosher salt

¼ teaspoon freshly ground black pepper

½ cup extra-virgin olive oil

Salad

8 ounces baby spinach, preferably local

2 medium strawberries, hulled, and sliced

2 tablespoons extra-virgin olive oil

1 teaspoon lemon zest

2 teaspoons fresh lemon juice

¼ teaspoon kosher salt, or to taste

¼ teaspoon freshly ground black pepper, or to taste

2 (2-ounce) balls fresh burrata cheese, cut in half, preferably Maplebrook Farm

½ cup shelled pistachios, salted and roasted

1 to 2 tablespoons aged balsamic vinegar, or to taste

1. To make the basil pesto: Place the basil and pine nuts into the bowl of a food processor and pulse several times. Add the Parmigiano-Reggiano, garlic, salt, and pepper, then pulse several times more. While the processor is running, slowly add the olive oil in a steady stream until well blended and fairly smooth, scraping down the sides of the bowl as needed.

2. To make the salad: In a large bowl, toss together the spinach and strawberries. In a small bowl, whisk together the olive oil, lemon zest and juice, salt, and pepper until well combined. Adjust seasonings with salt and pepper to taste. Drizzle over the salad, tossing until well coated.

3. To assemble: Smear the basil pesto onto a platter. Place the salad in the center of the platter. Place the burrata on top. Scatter the pistachios on and around the salad. Drizzle the balsamic vinegar on top and around the salad. Season with salt and pepper to taste. Serve at once.

Note: The pesto makes more than you will need for the salad, so freeze the extra for later use. Spoon the pesto into ice cube trays, then freeze until solid. Remove the pesto cubes from the trays and place in a freezer bag and freeze for up to 3 months.

The Reluctant Panther Inn and Restaurant/Executive Chef Sigal Rocklin

Honey Road is located at the intersection of Church and Main Street, in a bustling area of Burlington, Vermont. The restaurant's menu reflects the seasonal offerings from local farms.

Allison Gibson and Cara Chigazola Tobin are co-owners of the business, with Gibson taking on the role of general manager and Chigazola Tobin as executive chef. Chigazola Tobin began her restaurant career at the age of 17, working for a pizza establishment where the young chef learned how to operate a professional kitchen, familiarizing herself with its equipment and gaining organizational and efficiency skills. Moving forward, she worked as a line cook, baker, and brunch cook, as well as banquet, sous, and executive chef. Before moving to Vermont and becoming co-owner of Honey Road, Chigazola Tobin spent six years as chef de cuisine at Oleana in Cambridge, Massachusetts, a prestigious James Beard Award–winning restaurant.

Gibson has been working in the restaurant industry since age 14. At one point in her career, she was operations director for Hen of the Wood and Doc Ponds eateries. She met Chigazola Tobin in 2016, introduced by a mutual friend. It was during the women's second get-together that Chigazola Tobin asked Gibson if she would be interested in opening a restaurant with her. The answer was an immediate, "Yes!"

The women had no specific location in mind for their venture, eventually leasing the space that once housed Smokejacks in Burlington, Vermont. Gibson had been a server there and was familiar with the layout. After spending hours writing a business plan, the two women built a collaborative vision for their restaurant. They named the business Honey Road, a reference to a long-ago market in Kars, Turkey, where women took over beekeeping and related activities when the men went to war. Pop-up dinners were organized with the goal of presenting Chigazola Tobin's cuisine to the public, as well as introducing the chef to Vermont's restaurant community.

Honey Road opened its doors during the summer of 2017, serving small-plate savory dishes called "mezze." The atmosphere is comfortably casual yet refined. Its menu is simply arranged, with a section for dips and another for mezze. Because some items may require an explanation, a glossary is also included. All dishes are designed for sharing and are sent from the kitchen as soon as they are prepared. It is not unusual for two people to sometimes order as many as six small plates. For those who want their own meal, the restaurant offers a few selections that are large enough to be regular entrées. There is a widespread variety of culinary options to choose from—dishes from Greece, Turkey, and the Near and Middle East.

Gibson and Chigazola Tobin believe in buying local, supporting the area's small farms and businesses. With food sourced from area farms, both vegetarians and meat-eaters will be pleasantly surprised by the range of menu choices. During the winter months, many of the selections are vegetarian. Guests often include out-of-town visitors, chefs, and locals.

In 2018, Honey Road was nominated as a James Beard Foundation Award semifinalist for best new restaurant. Chigazola Tobin was nominated in 2018, 2019, and 2020 as a James Beard Foundation Award semifinalist in the best chef category. Honey Road, with its delightfully warm ambience, coupled with food that tantalizes your tastebuds, is truly a recipe for success.

Summer Fattoush Salad (Lebanese Summer Salad)

**SERVES 10 TO 12;
MAKES JUST OVER ⅔ CUP DRESSING**

Fattoush is a Lebanese bread salad that showcases the summer's bounty. This simple salad uses toasted pita bread instead of croutons. Make sure to add the toasted bread right before serving to ensure that the pita pieces stay crispy.

Pitas

2 (8-inch) pitas, torn into bite-sized pieces

¼ cup extra virgin olive oil

Lemon Dressing

3½ tablespoons fresh lemon juice

1 large garlic clove, pressed or minced

1 teaspoon honey, or to taste

1 teaspoon sumac plus ¼ teaspoon for garnish

1 teaspoon kosher salt

½ teaspoon freshly ground black pepper

½ cup extra-virgin olive oil

Salad

1 head Romaine lettuce, chopped into bite-sized pieces

6 ounces fennel bulb, trimmed, quartered, and thinly sliced or shaved (about 1 to 1¼ cups), reserving 2 tablespoons fennel fronds for garnish

1 cup hulled strawberries, sliced into bite-sized pieces

½ cup fresh blueberries

1¼ cups minced red onion

1 tablespoon roughly chopped fresh dill leaves, or to taste

1 tablespoon roughly chopped fresh parsley leaves, or to taste

1 tablespoon roughly chopped fresh mint leaves, or to taste

½ teaspoon kosher salt

¼ teaspoon freshly ground black pepper

1. Preheat the oven to 350°F. Line a baking sheet with parchment paper.

2. To make the pitas: Lay the pitas pieces on the baking sheet and toss with the olive oil until evenly coated. Bake in the oven until golden brown and crisp, about 12 minutes.

3. To make the lemon dressing: In a bowl, combine the lemon juice, garlic, honey, sumac, salt, and pepper until well combined. Add the oil in a slow and steady stream, whisking vigorously until emulsified. Adjust seasoning with additional honey, if desired, and salt and pepper to taste.

4. To make the salad: In a large bowl combine the lettuce, fennel, strawberries, blueberries, onion, dill, parsley, and mint. Add ⅓ cup of the dressing, ½ teaspoon salt, and ¼ teaspoon black pepper, tossing until well combined. Add the pita pieces, tossing until well combined. Adjust seasonings with additional dressing, if desired, and salt and pepper to taste. Garnish with sprinkles of sumac and fennel fronds on top and around the salad. Serve immediately with the remaining dressing at the table.

Note: The lemon dressing makes more than you will need for the salad. Drizzle the extra dressing over roasted vegetables, potatoes, or fish.

Honey Road

VEGETABLES

TWIN FARMS

The best of New England is brought to life at Twin Farms, the casually luxurious, exclusive retreat settled among lush Vermont mountains. Natural by design, the adults-only culinary destination exemplifies the new era of bespoke through its chef-guided culinary experience, richly appointed accommodations, museum-grade art collection, and a plethora of indoor and outdoor activities (i.e. axe throwing, archery, fly fishing, picnicking, Stave Puzling, etc.).

Executive Chef Nathan Rich and his apt team dream up new dishes daily for a menuless dining experience, leaning on Vermont's finest products sourced both on the property and with trusted local and regional partners to delight palates at Vermont's only five-star, all-inclusive Relais & Châteaux property.

Fall Root Vegetable Salad and Champagne Honey Vinaigrette

SERVES 4; MAKES ½ CUP DRESSING

This beautiful salad has a colorful array of fresh fall root vegetables. The earthy golden beets and celery root pairs beautifully with the mildly sweet carrots and cucumbers. The peppery notes from French breakfast radishes complements the other ingredients perfectly. The citrus flavor from the orange segments adds a nice layer of brightness, while the champagne honey vinaigrette lends a more subtle, sweet balance to the dish that really allows the salad ingredients to shine. See photo on page 60.

Fall Root Vegetable Salad

1 large golden beet

1 celery root (approximately ¾ pound)

1 medium carrot, sliced into ribbons

1 English cucumber, unpeeled
    and sliced into ribbons

2 French breakfast radishes

¼ cup crème fraîche

1 orange, pith and peel removed and cut into
    supremes (see Tip), reserving any juice

1 tablespoon sesame seeds, toasted

Fresh petit herbs, such as basil, mint,
    amaranth, chervil, or chive for garnish

Kosher salt and freshly ground black pepper

Champagne Honey Vinaigrette

6 tablespoons extra-virgin olive oil

2 tablespoons champagne vinegar

1 tablespoon honey

Kosher salt and freshly ground black pepper

1. To prepare the vegetables: Place the beet in a medium pot of cold salted water. Bring to a boil over medium-high heat, then reduce the temperature and simmer until you can easily insert a sharp knife into the center of beet. Drain thoroughly in a colander and set aside until cool enough to handle.

2. While the beet is simmering, wash and peel the celery root, carrot, and cucumber, reserving the skins for later use, such as a stock. Using a mandolin, thinly slice the celery root, carrot, and cucumber into thin ribbons. Set aside. Thinly slice the radishes long. See note below on how to produce ribbons.

3. Place the crème fraîche into a bowl and, using a handheld mixer, whip until soft peaks form. Set aside.

4. To prepare the champagne honey vinaigrette: In a bowl whisk together the olive oil, champagne vinegar, honey, salt, and pepper until well combined.

5. To assemble: Spoon some of the whipped crème fraîche onto the bottom of four bowls. Roll up the vegetable ribbons into tiny tubes, then gently press them into the crème fraîche. Drizzle with the champagne vinaigrette and reserved orange juice, to taste. Place the citrus segments around rolls. Sprinkle the sesame seeds over the top. For garnish, lightly scatter the petit herbs around and between the rolls. Sprinkle with salt and pepper to taste. Serve at once.

Note: To produce ribbons, using a mandolin or vegetable peeler, rotate the celery root, carrot, and cucumber on their axis a quarter turn after each ribbon is peeled. Continue until the vegetable is too small to handle, reserving the vegetable pieces for later use, such as a stock.

Twin Farms/Executive Chef Nathan Rich

TIP: HOW TO SUPREME AN ORANGE

Start by cutting off the ends of the orange. Using a sharp paring knife, starting at the top, slice as close to the orange flesh as possible to remove the pith and peel by following the curve of the orange in a downward motion. Once the peel and pith are removed, slice off any remaining pith. Hold the orange over a small bowl and cut the orange into supremes, discarding any membranes or seeds, and reserve the orange juice in the bowl.

GREEN MOUNTAIN GARLIC

In 1979, when Bob and Cindy Maynard first moved to Waterbury, they had no idea how much organic garlic would influence their lives. Over the years, Green Mountain Garlic has evolved from a home garden into what is now their current farm. After lengthy conversations with organic garlic farmers who sold seed garlic, the two realized that there was a need for organic garlic and decided to grow their own.

When the youngest of their three children left for college, the Maynards converted the old hay field on their 100-acre Waterbury property into an organic garlic farm. Today, the farm grows five varieties of hardneck and softneck garlic using organic and sustainable methods.

Winter Squash with Roasted Garlic

This side dish is both easy and satisfying with its creamy texture and mildly sweet, nutty flavors from the roasted butternut squash and garlic.

3¼ pounds butternut squash

4 tablespoons (2 ounces) unsalted butter, softened

1½ large garlic heads, roasted (recipe follows)

3½ tablespoons pure Vermont maple syrup

½ teaspoon freshly ground white pepper, plus extra

¼ teaspoon grated nutmeg

Kosher salt

1½ teaspoons minced fresh thyme leaves

1. Preheat the oven to 425°F.

2. Halve the squash lengthwise and remove the seeds and strings. Rub the inside of each half with 1 tablespoon butter. Place, skin side down, in a large roasting pan and add enough water to generously cover the bottom of pan. Roast until the flesh is fork-tender, about 45 minutes. Let stand until cool.

3. Meanwhile, squeeze the garlic flesh from the skins into a food processor.

4. When the squash is cool enough to handle, scoop out the flesh and place it in the food processor with the garlic. Add the remaining 2 tablespoons butter, maple syrup, ½ teaspoon pepper, and nutmeg, and purée until smooth. Season with salt and pepper to taste and pulse to incorporate. Transfer to a serving bowl, sprinkle with thyme, and serve.

Green Mountain Garlic

ROASTED GARLIC

This is one of the easiest and tastiest of garlic treats. Roasting caramelizes garlic slightly and makes it mild, sweet, and creamy in texture. It is wonderful as a spread, and can be used in a variety of dressings and sauces. You can substitute it in any dish that calls for garlic. What you don't use can be kept in the refrigerator for up to 10 days.

2 large garlic heads

Olive oil

Water

Preheat the oven to 350°F. Slice off the top portion of the heads and peel off just the outer papery layers of skin. Place the heads face up in a baking dish or garlic baker and sprinkle with oil and a bit of water. Bake until the cloves feel soft when pressed, about 1 hour.

Green Mountain Garlic

Braised Red Cabbage

SERVES 6 TO 8

The smell of this flavorful recipe takes chef Courtney Contos back to her childhood, all the way to her grandmother's kitchen in Germany. Today, Contos enjoys the braised red cabbage with beef rouladen, roast chicken, or pork. It is a great vegetable to make ahead.

2 tablespoons (1 ounce) unsalted butter

1 medium sweet onion, such as Vidalia or
    Walla Walla, thinly sliced

2 pounds red cabbage (1 medium head), shredded

Kosher salt and freshly ground black pepper

1½ cups fresh or frozen whole cranberries

1 cup Vermont apple cider

1 bay leaf

5 juniper berries

1 cinnamon stick

1 large tart apple, cored and diced

3 tablespoons dark brown sugar

3 tablespoons Vermont apple cider vinegar

1. Melt the butter in a large stockpot over medium heat. Add the onion and cook until tender and slightly translucent. Add the cabbage, 1 teaspoon salt, and ½ teaspoon pepper and sauté, stirring occasionally, for 5 minutes.

2. Add the cranberries, cider, bay leaf, juniper berries, and cinnamon stick. Cover and cook, stirring occasionally, until the cabbage is tender, about 1 hour.

3. Add the apple, sugar, and vinegar, stirring until well combined. Cover and continue cooking until the apple is very tender, about 10 minutes. Remove the bay leaf and cinnamon stick, season with salt and pepper to taste, and serve.

Courtney Contos

Cumin-Roasted Tri-Colored Carrots with Chèvre

SERVES 4

If you ask most people what color a carrot is, the immediate response is usually "orange." However, the very first carrots, which were grown over 1,000 years ago, were actually purple, red, and yellow. Today these many-colored carrots have made a comeback. They vary slightly in sweetness and crispness from standard orange carrots, but they can be prepared the same way. If you are unable to find rainbow carrots, your typical carrot will also work well for this dish.

12 medium to large rainbow carrots of assorted colors, scrubbed, thick ends halved lengthwise, and cut into 2-inch pieces

2 tablespoons olive oil

½ teaspoon ground cumin

1 teaspoon kosher salt

½ teaspoon freshly ground black pepper

1 tablespoon Vermont apple cider

1½ ounces goat cheese, crumbled (⅓ cup)

1 tablespoon minced fresh cilantro

1. Preheat the oven to 400°F. Lightly oil a baking sheet and set aside.

2. Place the carrots in a large bowl, add the olive oil, cumin, 1 teaspoon salt, and ½ teaspoon pepper and toss until evenly coated.

3. Place the carrots in a single layer on the prepared baking sheet. Drizzle any remaining oil and seasonings in the bowl over the carrots. Roast, tossing occasionally, until tender and golden brown, about 30 minutes.

4. Sprinkle the carrots with cider and toss to coat. Adjust seasonings with salt and pepper, if desired. Transfer the carrots to a platter and scatter the goat cheese and cilantro over the top. Serve.

Note: It is important to keep the carrot pieces a similar size so they finish cooking at the same time. This means that some ends may need to be quartered if necessary.

Tracey Medeiros

FOOTE BROOK FARM

Although Tony Lehouillier started Foote Brook Farm in 1997, his farming roots go back at least three generations. From 1955 to 1985, the site of the present Foote Brook farm was the Lehouillier Dairy Farm. Tony's mother, Polly Lehouillier, planted gardens, built greenhouses, and ran a farm stand out of the old dairy barn. Tony, along with some friends and partners, started out by growing a few varieties of vegetables and selling them to local restaurants, small co-ops, farmers' markets, and his mom's farm stand. Since then, Foote Brook Farm has grown to 45 acres producing 145 varieties of fruits and vegetables, sold at two farmers' markets, a retail stand, and through lots of small local accounts.

Tony and his wife, Joie, pride themselves on meeting the high standards of organic certification. Their employees (who call themselves Footebrookers) are the heart and soul of the farm. Every Friday the Lehouilliers look forward to sitting down with their staff and sharing the day's events and future plans, over some deliciously prepared farm-fresh food.

Grilled Coconut Delicata Squash

SERVES 4

This recipe, a family favorite, was inspired by the potential health benefits of coconut oil and the Lehouilliers' love of coconut, as well as their need for dishes that are simple enough to make.

2 pounds delicata squash (about 3 medium) halved lengthwise, seeded, and cut crosswise into ½-inch-wide slices
¼ cup organic extra-virgin coconut oil
Kosher salt
⅓ cup shredded coconut, toasted

1. Toss the squash with the coconut oil in a medium bowl and season with salt to taste.

2. Heat a grill to medium-high and grill the squash until tender, about 3 minutes per side. Top with the shredded coconut and serve.

Foote Brook Farm

Stuffed Collard Greens

SERVES 6

These stuffed collard greens were first prepared for one of the Friday afternoon Footebrookers' meals. The collard greens' versatility makes it possible to stuff the leaves with a variety of local products.

1 tablespoon olive oil

2 medium onions or 1 bunch white early bunching onions with greens, chopped

2 (4-ounce) links sweet or spicy sausage, casings removed

1 bunch collard greens, stems removed

2 cups whole-milk ricotta cheese

1 large garlic clove, minced

5 plum tomatoes, chopped

1. Preheat the oven to 350°F. Lightly oil a 9 x 13-inch baking pan and set aside. Fill a large bowl with ice water and set aside.

2. Heat the oil in a medium skillet over medium heat. Add the onions and sauté until soft and translucent. Add the sausage and cook, crumbling with a fork, until browned, about 7 minutes.

3. Meanwhile, fill a 6-quart stockpot halfway with water and bring to a boil over medium-high heat. Add the collards and blanch for 2 to 3 minutes. Using a slotted spoon, transfer the collards to the prepared ice bath and let cool completely. Drain the collards thoroughly and pat dry with paper towels.

4. Working in batches, lay the collard greens out on a work surface. Stir the ricotta and garlic together to blend and then spread a thin layer of the ricotta mixture on one side of each collard leaf. Spread about 2 tablespoons of the sausage mixture over the cheese.

5. Loosely roll up the collard greens lengthwise, being careful to keep the mixture inside of each bundle; carefully tie each roll with butcher's twine, securing the ends and center portion to form an oblong roll, or secure with toothpicks. Transfer to the prepared pan. Top with the tomatoes and bake for 25 minutes. Serve.

Foote Brook Farm

VALLEY DREAM FARM

Valley Dream Farm is located in an area of Cambridge, Vermont, known as "Pleasant Valley." Majestic Mount Mansfield overlooks the picturesque, diversified organic produce farm. Its owners, Joe and Anne Tisbert, believe in being good stewards of the land, protecting the environment by using sustainable farming techniques. This is the 10th year that the Tisbert's have offered their farm-to-table "chef's dinner." Many of the guest have returned year after year for the delicious seasonal meal, highlighted by a hayride farm tour. The event is always met with words of praise and a promise to return. The agriculturally preserved farm has received awards for its generous donations to local food shelves. The Tisbert's are working to help build a better, stronger community by encouraging and inspiring those who live there to support the greater good. It is easy to understand why this area of Vermont is known as Pleasant Valley!

Roasted Roots

SERVES 8

Feel free to alter the amounts in the seasoning mix to suit your taste, and to experiment with other root vegetables such as rutabagas, sweet potatoes, and garlic. There is no need to peel the potatoes, turnips, parsnips, or carrots. To ensure even cooking, cut the vegetables so they are uniform in size. Leftovers taste great reheated or added to soup.

8 ounces red beets, cut into 1-inch pieces

8 ounces red potatoes, cut into 1-inch pieces

8 ounces golden turnips, cut into 1-inch pieces

8 ounces parsnips, cut diagonally into 1-inch pieces

8 ounces carrots, cut diagonally into 1-inch pieces

1 small onion, cut into ⅓-inch wedges

3 garlic cloves, sliced

1 tablespoon chopped fresh parsley,
    plus extra for sprinkling

1 teaspoon chopped fresh thyme,
    plus extra for sprinkling

1 teaspoon chopped fresh rosemary,
    plus extra for sprinkling

½ teaspoon garlic salt

Salt and freshly ground black pepper

¼ cup olive oil

1. Preheat the oven to 400°F. Lightly oil a 9 x 13-inch baking dish and set aside.

2. Place the beets, potatoes, turnips, parsnips, carrots, onion, garlic, parsley, thyme, rosemary, garlic salt, and ¼ teaspoon pepper in a large bowl. Drizzle the oil over the vegetables and toss to combine, making sure to coat all the vegetables well.

3. Spread the vegetable mixture into the prepared baking dish. Roast, stirring every 15 minutes, until the vegetables are fork-tender and golden brown, 45 to 50 minutes.

4. Season with salt and pepper to taste. Sprinkle with additional parsley, thyme, and rosemary and serve.

Valley Dream Farm

LAZY LADY FARM

Lazy Lady Farm, owned by Laini Fondiller, is in the town of Westfield, near the Canadian border. When Fondiller graduated from college she wanted to try something new, so she went to work on dairy farms. In 1981, she traveled to Corsica, France, where she stumbled into the cheesemaking business, and her love of cheese began. Fondiller remained in France for over two years, working at various goat cheese operations where she honed her craft.

When she returned home, Fondiller began adapting the recipes she had learned to make her own cheeses. She has been making cheese for more than 34 years now, milking more than 40 registered Alpine goats and producing more than 10,000 pounds of cheese a year. Fondiller's interest in politics has moved her to give many of her cheeses politically inspired names.

THE PITCHER INN

The Pitcher Inn has been welcoming guests since the early 1850s. It was originally a simple country inn where weary travelers who ventured over treacherous mountain paths from Granville, Lincoln, or Roxbury would stop to rest. The inn has evolved over the decades, providing hearty meals and welcoming guests who vacation in the quaint, quiet village of Warren. It is affiliated with Relais & Châteaux, the international association of luxury hotels and restaurants.

Today's Pitcher Inn epitomizes hospitality, grace, and Vermont charm. Each room represents select aspects of the state; its history, character, sports, and social structure are all intertwined with the comforts discerning travelers expect of a small luxury hotel.

The inn's restaurants, The Dining Rooms & Tracks, have also grown with the times. Vermont and the Mad River Valley boast an amazing variety of farmers, artisanal cheesemakers, orchards, apiaries, and breweries. This diversity of incredible products provides inspiration for executive chef Jacob Ennis, chef de cuisine Peter Heaney, and their culinary team. Both the inn's restaurants rely on fresh, seasonal ingredients and are supported by a wine cellar boasting more than 500 selections.

Spring Pea Soup

SERVES 6 TO 8

This light, fresh pea soup is just as delicious served hot, at room temperature, or chilled. If fresh peas are not available, use frozen—just remember to thaw and rinse them before use.

Mushrooms

½ pound local wild mushrooms, cleaned, trimmed, and cut into 1-inch pieces

½ teaspoon kosher salt

Pea Soup

1 tablespoon unsalted butter

¼ pound shallots, finely chopped

3 fresh ramp leaves, coarsely chopped, or 1 cup leeks white and green parts, coarsely chopped

½ gallon (8 cups) vegetable broth

1½ pounds fresh peas, shelled or frozen, thawed and rinsed

1¼ teaspoons kosher salt, or to taste

½ teaspoon freshly ground black pepper, or to taste

Garnishes

Whipped crème fraîche

Pickled red onions, store-bought or homemade

Microgreens

Crusty bread (optional)

1. To make the mushrooms: Heat a dry carbon steel fry pan over medium heat. Add the mushrooms, being careful not to overcrowd. Dry sauté the mushrooms until they become fragrant and turn a nice golden brown. Sprinkle with salt, tossing until evenly coated. then transfer to a bowl until ready to use as a garnish.

2. Place a large bowl of ice water near your cooking area. Set a large bowl on top of the prepared ice bath.

3. To prepare the pea soup: Melt the butter in a large stockpot or Dutch oven over medium heat. Add the shallots and ramp leaves, if using, and cook over medium heat until tender, about 5 minutes.

4. Add the vegetable broth, then increase the heat to medium-high, and bring to a boil.

5. Add the peas and cook until tender, about 3 minutes.

6. Remove from the heat, add the salt and pepper, stirring until well combined. Working in batches, place the soup in a blender and blend until smooth.

7. Carefully pour the soup into the large bowl resting on top of the prepared ice bath. Stir the soup frequently, for 3 minutes. As you blend the soup, pour the contents of each batch directly into the chilled bowl resting on top of the prepared ice bath. This will ensure that the soup will maintain its beautiful green color. Repeat with the remaining ingredients. Adjust seasonings with salt and pepper to taste.

8. To assemble: Ladle into soup bowls, then top with a dollop of crème fraîche. Scatter the reserved mushrooms, red onions, and microgreens around the soup. Serve with crusty bread on the side, if desired.

Note: When blending hot liquids, always fill the blender jar halfway, remove the lid's center insert, and place a kitchen towel over the top, holding it securely, then blend. This will help avoid a soup explosion.

The Pitcher Inn

SQUARE DEAL FARM

In 1997, when Sarah Lyons and Ray Lewis bought their 146-acre farm in Walden, their dream was to develop the property for maple sugaring. The husband and wife team started off on a very small scale with approximately 250 taps. Today, the farm has around 6,000 taps. In addition to their maple sugar operation, they raise Pinzgauer cattle.

Lyons and Lewis believe in the importance of sustainable agriculture and their dedication to the organic community is seen in every aspect of their farming practices. The farm's maple syrup and sugar are VOF-certified organic. This means that every step along the way has been checked to ensure that the farm manages their sugarbush sustainably without the use of chemicals or pesticides. Everything that comes in contact with their sap, syrup, and sugar must conform to rigorous standards.

Maple-Glazed Sweet Potatoes

SERVES 6

To give the potatoes a richer caramelized look, after baking, place them under the broiler for 3 to 5 minutes.

3 medium sweet potatoes (about 2 pounds), scrubbed well

3 tablespoons (1½ ounces) unsalted butter

¼ cup pure Vermont maple syrup

1 teaspoon ground cumin

⅓ cup chopped walnuts

Sea salt and freshly ground black pepper

2–3 tablespoons thinly sliced scallions

Grated nutmeg

1. Preheat the oven to 350°F. Lightly grease a 9-inch square or 7 x 11-inch baking pan and set aside.

2. Place the sweet potatoes in a large pot of cold salted water. Bring to a boil over medium-high heat, then reduce the temperature and simmer until the potatoes are fork-tender, 20 to 30 minutes. Drain thoroughly in a colander and set aside.

3. When the potatoes are cool enough to handle, peel and cut them into 2-inch chunks. Place the potato chunks in a single layer in the prepared pan.

4. In a small saucepan, combine the butter, maple syrup, and cumin over medium-low heat, and simmer, stirring occasionally, for 3 minutes. Pour the maple mixture over the sweet potatoes and toss to coat evenly. Top the mixture with the walnuts and season with salt and pepper to taste. Bake until tender and lightly golden, 10 to 15 minutes. Sprinkle with the scallions and nutmeg to taste, and serve.

Square Deal Farm

FARMER SUE'S FARM

Farmer Sue's Farm is on 15 acres in Bakersfield, not far from the Canadian border. Sue Wells and her son Ben grow vegetables using organic standards and grain to feed their pigs and a flock of more than a hundred chickens. The pigs include unusual heritage breeds—Red Wattle (named for both its color and its distinctive wattles) and American Mulefoot—both considered critically endangered by the American Livestock Breeds Conservancy.

Pickled Cucumber and Sweet Onion Salad

SERVES 4 TO 6

It's best to use English cucumbers or pickling cucumbers in this salad, because their skins are not waxed.

½ cup water

¼ cup Vermont apple cider vinegar

2 tablespoons granulated sugar

2 tablespoons extra-virgin olive oil

1 teaspoon finely chopped fresh basil

1 teaspoon celery seeds

1 teaspoon coriander seeds

Kosher salt and freshly ground black pepper

1 large English cucumber or 1 to 1¼ pounds pickling cucumbers

1 small sweet onion, such as Vidalia or Walla Walla, thinly sliced

Fresh chopped dill for garnish

1. In a small bowl, whisk together the water, vinegar, sugar, oil, basil, celery seeds, coriander seeds, and salt and pepper to taste.

2. Remove the peel from the cucumber in long strips, leaving narrow, decorative stripes of peel attached. Thinly slice the cucumber into rounds. Place the cucumber and onion in a large, shallow dish, pour the marinade over the vegetables, and toss to coat. Cover with plastic wrap and refrigerate, turning occasionally, for at least 12 hours or overnight. Garnish with dill and serve, using a slotted spoon.

Sue Wells for the Burlington Farmers' Market

BURLINGTON FARMERS' MARKET

The Burlington Farmers' Market has been operating for over 40 years in downtown Burlington. Every Saturday, the market hosts more than 90 vendors whose stands overflow with seasonal produce, flowers, artisan-crafted goods, prepared foods, and much more. The market bustles with locals and visitors enjoying shopping local and supporting small businesses. Every one of the products available at the market is produced, grown, and crafted in the state of Vermont.

Zucchini Spread

MAKES 3 CUPS

Since zucchini has a very high water content, it is important to squeeze out as much moisture as possible before processing it. Serve this spread with crackers, bread rounds, or fresh raw vegetables.

3 cups finely shredded zucchini (about 2 medium zucchini)

8 ounces reduced-fat cream cheese, softened

¼ cup chopped fresh cilantro

2 tablespoons extra-virgin olive oil

2 tablespoons lemon juice plus ½ teaspoon grated lemon zest

1 tablespoon grated Parmesan cheese

2 garlic cloves, minced

Salt and freshly ground white pepper

1. Wrap the zucchini in a clean dish towel and squeeze out the excess moisture. Process the zucchini, cream cheese, cilantro, oil, lemon juice, Parmesan, and garlic in a food processor until smooth, scraping down the sides of the bowl as needed. Spoon the mixture into a serving bowl, cover, and refrigerate for at least 1 hour or overnight.

2. Season the spread with salt and pepper to taste, sprinkle with lemon zest, and serve.

Sue Wells for the Burlington Farmers' Market

POMYKALA FARM

Pomykala Farm is a small family-run operation located on the Lake Champlain Islands in northern Vermont. The owners, Bob and Jane Pomykala, purchased their first piece of farmland in 1981, and their second in 1989. They felt that the islands were an ideal place to grow crops because Lake Champlain offers tempering effects from the extremes of weather. The lake holds the heat, which helps to make their fall last longer. The Pomykalas grow fruits, vegetables, herbs, and flowers on 25 acres. They also cultivate row crops and use cover crops to blanket out weeds, improve soil production, and build fertility.

Asparagus and Brown Rice

MAKES 6 CUPS; SERVES 4 AS A MAIN COURSE OR 6 AS A SIDE DISH

Jane Pomykala, co-owner of Pomykala Farm, likes to make this hearty meal in spring, when asparagus first appears on the scene. This simple dish is bright with citrus notes from the lemon zest and juice, as well as a subtle nuttiness from the brown rice and Parmesan cheese.

1½ cups short- or medium-grain brown rice

3½ cups low-sodium chicken broth

1 tablespoon unsalted butter

1½ pounds asparagus, trimmed and sliced diagonally into 1-inch pieces

1 small bunch scallions, white and green parts, chopped (about 1 cup)

1 ounce Parmesan cheese, grated (½ cup)

1 teaspoon grated lemon zest

1 tablespoon lemon juice

½ teaspoon kosher salt

¼ teaspoon freshly ground black pepper

1½ teaspoons chopped fresh thyme

1. Place the rice in a fine-mesh strainer and rinse thoroughly. Place the rice and broth in a medium saucepan and bring to a simmer over medium heat. Cover tightly, reduce the heat to low, and cook until tender and most of the liquid has been absorbed, 50 minutes.

2. Melt the butter in a medium skillet over medium heat. Add the asparagus and scallions and sauté, stirring occasionally until tender, 6 to 8 minutes. Transfer to a medium bowl and add the rice. Stir in the Parmesan and lemon zest and juice. Season with salt and pepper to taste, sprinkle with thyme, and serve.

Pomykala Farm

NEW LEAF ORGANICS

New Leaf Organics is located in the Champlain Valley, on the town line between Bristol and Monkton. In 2001, Jill Kopel began transforming what had been a small dairy farm for many years into an organic vegetable and flower farm. Of the 90-acre farm, 4 acres of land are in production and mostly devoted to vegetables. The flower gardens are beautiful and give inspiration to visitors. Every "flattish" piece of ground is planted during the growing season. The rest of the farm sits high above the road offering great views of Hogback Ridge. People who live within a 20-mile radius of the farm enjoy most of the food they produce. New Leaf Organics offers CSA shares, participates in two farmers' markets, and has wholesale accounts in Middlebury and Burlington. Their farm stand offers mostly vegetable, herb, and flower plants in the spring and then produce when it becomes available. Their flowers show up at events throughout Chittenden and Addison counties. New Leaf is a labor of love for Kopel, her husband, Skimmer Hellier, and their children, Ruby and Ada.

Spring Frittata

SERVES 6

This is one of the Kopel family's favorite breakfast recipes. It is delicate and creamy, with subtle layers of flavor. Any slightly tangy, full-bodied raw-milk cheese can be used in place of the farmhouse cheese here.

3 medium yellow potatoes, quartered and
    thinly sliced

Kosher salt and freshly ground black pepper

7 large eggs, lightly beaten

½ teaspoon chopped fresh rosemary,
    plus extra for garnish

½ teaspoon chopped fresh sage,
    plus extra for garnish

2 tablespoons (1 ounce) unsalted butter

1 small zucchini, finely diced

1 large shallot, minced (about 3 tablespoons)

3 garlic cloves, minced

8 ounces baby spinach leaves, rinsed, dried, and
    coarsely chopped

3 ounces farmhouse-style cheese of choice,
    crumbled (¾ cup)

1½ ounces Grana Padano cheese, grated (¾ cup)

1. Combine the potatoes and ½ teaspoon salt in a medium saucepan, cover with cold water, and bring to a boil over medium-high heat. Cook until the potatoes are just tender, about 10 minutes. Drain in a colander and set aside.

2. In a medium bowl, whisk together the eggs, rosemary, sage, and salt and pepper to taste.

3. Adjust an oven rack to the top position and heat the broiler. Melt the butter in a 12-inch broiler-proof nonstick skillet over medium heat. Add the zucchini and cook until tender, about 5 minutes. Add the shallots and garlic and cook until soft and translucent, about 3 minutes. Add the spinach and cook until just wilted, about 2 minutes. Add the potatoes and cook for 2 minutes more.

4. Spread the vegetables evenly over the bottom of the pan. Pour the egg mixture over the vegetables. Using a spatula, gently lift up the vegetable mixture along the sides of the skillet to allow the egg mixture to flow underneath. Sprinkle with the farmhouse cheese. Reduce the heat to medium-low and cook until the frittata is almost set but still slightly runny.

5. Place the skillet under the broiler and broil until the frittata is puffed and golden brown, about 3 minutes. Let rest for 5 minutes, then, using a rubber spatula, loosen the frittata from the skillet and carefully slide onto a platter. Top with the Grana Padano cheese. Cut into wedges, sprinkle with rosemary and sage, and serve.

New Leaf Organics

Fresh "Springy" Spring Rolls

MAKES 12 LARGE ROLLS, SERVING 6

This recipe is one of Jill Kopel's go-to appetizers. Spring rolls are really fun to make with kids. It is a great way to get them to eat more green veggies, without realizing it! Serve these spring rolls with your favorite Asian-style dipping sauce, such as duck sauce or a soy-ginger sauce, and sliced avocado on the side, if desired.

2 ounces cellophane noodles

1 tablespoon safflower oil

1 large sweet onion, minced

3 heads baby pak choy, chopped

3–4 tablespoons tamari

3 garlic cloves, minced

3 carrots, peeled and shredded

1 cup shredded salad turnips

5 scallions, thinly sliced

1 tablespoon grated ginger

1 teaspoon rice vinegar

12 rice-paper wrappers

3 cups microgreens

¼ cup chopped fresh cilantro

¼ cup chopped fresh mint

¼ cup chopped dry-roasted peanuts

1 tablespoon sesame oil

1. Place the noodles in a large bowl and pour in enough hot water to cover. Let the noodles soak until they are soft and flexible, about 30 minutes. Drain, cut into 1½-inch lengths, and set aside.

2. Heat the oil in a medium skillet over medium heat. Add the onions and sauté, stirring often until soft, about 5 minutes. Add the pak choy, tamari, and garlic and sauté, stirring often, until soft, about 5 minutes. Remove from the heat and let cool completely.

3. In a medium bowl, combine the carrots, turnips, scallions, ginger, and rice vinegar.

4. Heat 2 cups water in a medium saucepan until hot but not boiling. Add 1 rice-paper wrapper, turning occasionally until softened, about 30 seconds. Using a slotted spoon, remove the wrapper and lay flat on clean, dry kitchen towels. Repeat with the remaining wrappers.

5. Place ¼ cup microgreens on each wrapper. Place about 1 tablespoon of the onion mixture and 1 tablespoon of the carrot mixture on the greens. Divide the cilantro, mint, peanuts, and sesame oil among the wrappers and top each wrapper with some noodles.

6. Working one at a time, fold the bottom of each wrapper up over the filling and roll into a tight cylinder, folding in the sides as you go. Place the rolls, seam side down, on a plate. Cover with a damp towel until ready to serve.

New Leaf Organics

WARREN STORE

The Warren Store was built in 1839, as a midway stagecoach stop between Boston and Montreal. It is nestled in picturesque Warren, in the Mad River Valley. Fun and always funky, Warren Store wears many different hats. First and foremost, the store is the social hub of the community and a favorite meeting place of locals and visitors alike.

The store has a wonderful deli and bakery where all of the products are made from scratch, using local ingredients whenever possible. There is also an award-winning wine shop and a boutique that showcases an array of men's and women's clothing (both fashionable and functional), accessories, jewelry, toys, and housewares.

Fennel Choucroute

MAKES 6 CUPS

Choucroute is French for sauerkraut. "We use fennel choucroute on our Reuben sandwich, making it as unique as it is delicious. The fresh flavor elevates the sandwich to a new level setting it apart from the usual fare," says executive chef Jacob Ennis.

Sachet

3 tablespoons whole caraway seeds

3 sprigs of thyme

½ teaspoon whole juniper berries

1 bay leaf

1 (6 x 6-inch) cheesecloth square

Butcher's twine as needed

Fennel Choucroute

1 tablespoon unsalted butter

½ pound slab smoked meaty bacon, nitrate-free, trimmed and diced

1 pound onions, trimmed and thinly sliced (about 2½ cups)

3 pounds fennel, bulbs trimmed, quartered, and thinly sliced or shaved (about 7½ cups), reserving 1 tablespoon coarsely chopped fennel fronds for garnish

1 cup apple cider vinegar

¼ cup dry white wine, such as Riesling

½ teaspoon kosher salt

¼ teaspoon freshly ground black pepper

1. Preheat the oven to 350°F

2. To make the sachet: Place the caraway seeds, thyme, juniper berries, and bay leaf in the center of a 6 x 6-inch cheesecloth square. Gather up the corners of the cheesecloth to form a bundle and tie tightly and securely with butcher's twine. Set aside.

3. To make the fennel choucroute: Heat the butter in a Dutch oven over medium heat. Add the bacon and cook, stirring often, until crisp. Using a slotted spoon, transfer the bacon to a paper towel–lined plate, reserving the drippings in the pan.

4. Add the onions and sauté until just soft, about 5 minutes. Reduce the heat to low, then add the fennel and sachet. Cook, stirring often for 5 minutes. Return the bacon to the pot and stir once more. Add the apple cider vinegar, wine, salt, and pepper, stirring until well combined.

5. Cover and bake in the oven until the onions and fennel are tender, about 60 minutes, depending on the size of the onion and fennel slices.

6. Strain through a fine mesh strainer, discarding the sachet. Adjust seasonings with salt and pepper to taste. Garnish with fronds over the top. Serve as you would sauerkraut, such as a topping on a juicy classic burger patty or on a traditional hotdog.

Note: The choucroute can be stored in an airtight container in the refrigerator for up to 3 days.

Warren Store

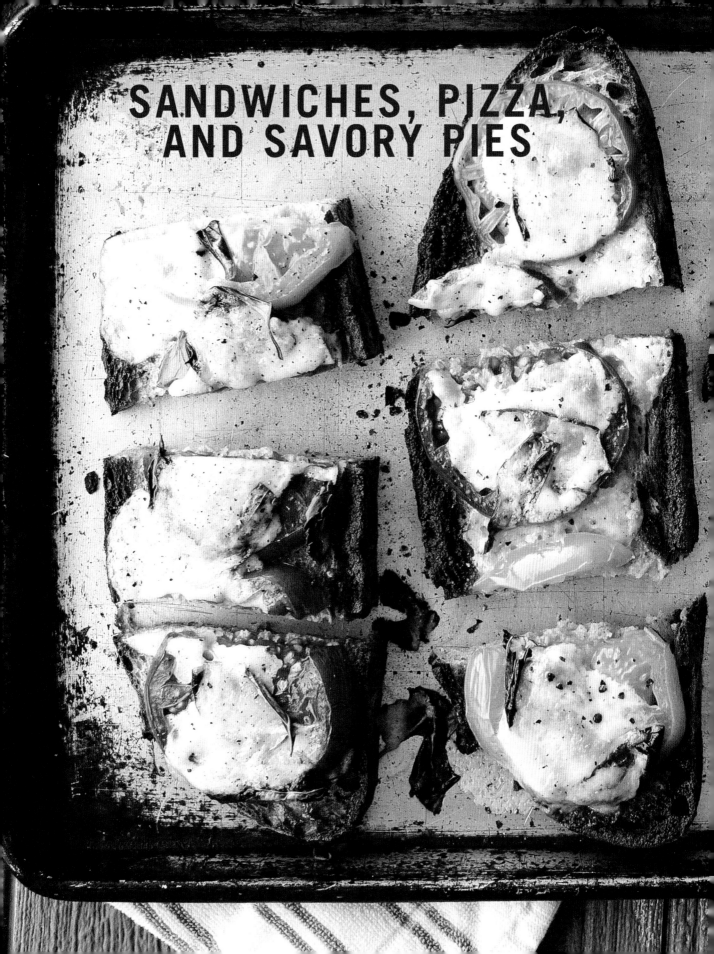

SANDWICHES, PIZZA, AND SAVORY PIES

FULL MOON FARM

Rachel Nevitt and David Zuckerman farm with a passion, growing great food in a responsible way. Their farm, Full Moon Farm, is a stunning 155-acre diversified farm located in Hinesburg. Nevitt and Zuckerman grow 40 to 45 fruits and vegetables, ranging from beautiful heirloom tomatoes to fragrant muskmelons, sweet corn to daikon radishes, all VOF-certified. The husband-and-wife team also raises certified organic pastured pork and certified organic pastured chickens, which they sell to their CSA members, as well as at the Burlington Farmers' Market, and, occasionally, wholesale. Occasionally, they offer their meat for wholesale, giving the lucky consumer a rare opportunity to enjoy their products. Nevitt and Zuckerman strongly feel that it is important for people to meet the farmers who use the best organic practices to grow their food. As they say, "We are absolutely committed to connecting consumers to their local food sources and producers."

Rachel's Caprese Sandwich with Heirloom Tomatoes, Extra-Sharp Cheddar Cheese, and Basil

SERVES 4

At Full Moon Farm this sandwich is made with bread from Good Companion Bakery (in nearby Vergennes), extra-sharp cheddar cheese from Cabot Creamery, and heirloom tomatoes and basil from the farm. This sandwich is also called "Rachel's Summer Joy." It makes a delicious luncheon dish and is ideal for a hearty snack. See photo on page 87.

4 slices ½-inch-thick rustic farm bread

4 ounces extra-sharp cheddar cheese, thinly sliced

**2–3 large heirloom tomatoes,
    cut into ⅓-inch-thick slices**

8–16 large basil leaves, torn into pieces

Olive oil

Salt and freshly ground black pepper

1. Adjust an oven rack to the top position and heat the broiler. Lightly toast the bread slices. Layer the tomato slices, basil leaves, and cheddar cheese on each slice. Drizzle with olive oil and season with salt and pepper to taste.

2. Place the sandwiches on a baking sheet and broil them until the cheese melts. Serve.

*David Zuckerman and Rachel Nevitt
of Full Moon Farm.*

CONSIDER BARDWELL FARM

Consider Bardwell Farm, located in West Pawlet, is a 300-acre goat and cow dairy farm, as well as an artisan cheesemaking operation. Consider Stebbins Bardwell founded the farm in 1864; it was the first cheesemaking co-op in Vermont. During the 1860s, local farmers would bring all their morning milk to the farm where it was made into cheese, which was later shipped to Albany, New York, and the Boston area.

In 2000, Angela Miller and her husband, Russell Glover, purchased the farm. They had a plan to revitalize the tradition of helping small, local farmers process their milk into cheese. The couple bought goats in 2002, and with the help of cheesemaker Peter Dixon, started experimenting with goat's milk cheese. The farm was officially licensed to sell cheese in 2004.

Today, post Covid pandemic, the farm makes only three kinds of cow's milk cheese from their own herd of 17 Jersey cows, milked at nearby Indian River Farm (one of the original farms of the 1860s co-op). All of their cheeses are made from raw milk, except for Dorset, their washed rind, French-style tomme. The farm has four aging caves where cheeses are aged for two months to two years.

All of the farm's cheeses are made by hand, in small batches, from milk that is antibiotic- and hormone-free and from cows that are pasture-based. The cheeses have all been named after places located around Consider Bardwell Farm— Dorset, Pawlet, and Rupert. All of the cheeses have earned national and international awards for excellence. Currently, the farm has two cheesemakers and produces 30,000 pounds of cheese a year.

Pawletti

MAKES 1 SANDWICH, SERVING 1 TO 2

The key to the success of this dish is high-quality ingredients. This mouthwatering sandwich is prepared with a rustic peasant-style bread and the farm's very own prize-winning raw Jersey cow's milk cheese, called Pawlet. It's their version of a panini. They offer it with organic bread-and-butter pickles and sliced apple, or with thin slices of onion, tomato, and prosciutto. Mustard is served on the side, of course.

1½ teaspoons unsalted butter, softened

2 slices rustic peasant bread

3 thin slices sweet onion

3 thin slices tomato

1–2 thin slices prosciutto

Freshly ground black pepper

1 (3-ounce) slice Pawlet cheese or any other mild raw cow's milk cheese

Coarse-grain or Dijon mustard

1. Preheat a grill pan over medium-high heat or preheat a panini press. Spread one side of each slice of bread with butter and place buttered side down on a cutting board. Layer one side of the bread with the onion, tomato, and prosciutto. Season with pepper to taste. Top with the cheese and the second slice of bread.

2. Place the sandwich on the grill pan or panini press. If using a pan, weigh down with a heavy skillet and cook until golden brown and the cheese has melted, 3 to 4 minutes per side. If using a panini press, grill according to the manufacturer's directions. Cut the sandwich in half and serve immediately, with mustard on the side.

Angela Miller of Consider Bardwell Farm

AMERICAN FLATBREAD COMPANY

In 1985, George Schenk constructed an outdoor stone oven and tried making flatbread. The experiment was a success and a new business was born. Two years later, he built an American Flatbread Bakery at Lareau Farm, a late 18th-century farm in Waitsfield, in the Mad River Valley. Since then, the franchise has expanded to include restaurants in Middlebury, Burlington, and 14 other locations, as well as a frozen flatbread business. In 2001, the company purchased the Inn at Lareau Farm, which is once again a working farm.

Through its years of growth, American Flatbread has kept the same goals: to create simple, wholesome flatbreads baked in a primitive, wood-fired earthen oven, and to feature organic ingredients raised and harvested by local farmers. By focusing on a simple menu, the restaurants can explore the boundaries of artisanal pizza making while maintaining the quality and integrity of what they serve. And by partnering with neighboring farmers, the company has been able to establish a sustainable, community-based farm-to-plate network.

Harvest Flatbread

SERVES 4 TO 6

This pizza is inspired by ingredients that are common in Vermont, such as new potatoes, tender spinach, smoked bacon, sweet maple syrup, and sharp cheddar cheese. If you don't own a pizza stone, you can use a flat (or upside down rimmed) baking sheet. A baking sheet or cutting board can also stand in for a pizza peel.

2 tablespoons unsalted butter

1 large sweet onion, thinly sliced

Kosher salt and freshly ground black pepper

1¼ pounds new potatoes (red or gold), thinly sliced

2 tablespoons olive oil

5 slices uncured bacon

Coarse cornmeal, as needed

1 pound prepared pizza dough, preferably organic

Garlic-Infused Olive Oil (recipe follows)

2 cups packed fresh baby spinach

2 cups shredded roasted or grilled chicken breast (about 3 chicken breasts)

8 ounces sharp or extra-sharp Vermont cheddar cheese, shredded (2 cups)

1 ounce Parmesan cheese, grated (½ cup)

Pure Vermont maple syrup

1. Position the oven racks in the upper third and lower third of the oven and place a baking stone on the rack. Preheat the oven to 450°F. (The stone should preheat for 45 minutes.)

2. Melt the butter in a large skillet over medium heat. Add the onion and stir to coat. Spread into an even layer and cook, stirring occasionally, for 10 minutes. Sprinkle with salt to taste, reduce the heat to medium-low, and cook until the onion is nicely browned, about 30 minutes.

3. Meanwhile, place the potatoes in a medium bowl and drizzle with oil; toss to coat well. Season with salt and pepper. Spread the potatoes onto a baking sheet and roast on the lower oven rack, stirring halfway through, until the potatoes are fork-tender, 20 to 25 minutes.

4. Cook the bacon in a medium skillet over medium-high heat until lightly cooked, about 3 minutes. Transfer to paper towels to drain. Coarsely chop the bacon.

5. Sprinkle cornmeal onto a pizza peel and place the dough on the peel. Using your hands, stretch the dough into a 14 x 16-inch rectangle, and brush with garlic-infused oil to taste. Season lightly with salt. Arrange the potatoes evenly over the dough, leaving a 1-inch border, then layer the spinach and onions over the potatoes. Sprinkle evenly with the chicken and bacon, then sprinkle the cheddar and Parmesan over the top. Drizzle the entire pizza with maple syrup.

6. Slide the pizza onto the baking stone and bake until the edge of the crust is lightly crisp and the cheese is lightly browned, 20 to 25 minutes.

American Flatbread Company

GARLIC-INFUSED OLIVE OIL

MAKES ½ CUP

½ cup extra-virgin olive oil

4 garlic cloves, thinly sliced

Heat the oil in a small saucepan over medium heat. Add the garlic and cook until fragrant, but not browned, 2 to 3 minutes. Let the oil cool, then cover and let steep for 1 hour. Strain the oil into a sterilized jar or bottle; discard the garlic. Use within 24 hours.

American Flatbread Company

KNOLL FARM

Knoll Farm is based in the Mad River Valley of central Vermont. The farm is known for raising purebred Icelandic Sheep and certified organic pick-your-own blueberries. Knoll Farm is also home of The Refuge at Knoll Farm, a retreat center well known nationally as a place where leadership, relationships, and well-being are given space to flourish.

Blueberry Goat Cheese Pizza with Caramelized Onions and Rosemary

SERVES 4 TO 6

One of Knoll Farm's signature dishes is a wood-fired blueberry, goat cheese, rosemary pizza, which is made in their outdoor mud oven. The pizza has a nice combination of sweet and savory. It has a creamy tang from the goat cheese (Knoll Farm uses fresh goat cheese from Vermont Creamery) and a sweet earthiness from caramelized onions coupled with blueberries. All of these ingredients, combined with the woody pine flavor from the fresh rosemary, make this pizza a real treat. If you don't own a pizza stone, you can use a flat (or upside-down rimmed) baking sheet. A baking sheet or cutting board can also stand in for a pizza peel.

3 tablespoons (1½ ounces) unsalted butter

2 large sweet onions, sliced thin

Kosher salt

Coarse cornmeal, as needed

1 pound pizza dough, preferably whole-wheat

2 tablespoons olive oil, or as needed

8 ounces fresh goat cheese, crumbled, at room temperature (2 cups)

1½ pints blueberries

3 tablespoons chopped fresh rosemary

Vermont honey

1. Place a baking stone in the oven and preheat the oven to 450°F. (The stone should preheat for 45 minutes.)

2. Melt the butter in a large skillet over medium heat. Add the onions and stir to coat. Spread the onions into an even layer and cook, stirring occasionally, for 10 minutes. Sprinkle with salt to taste, reduce the heat to medium-low, and cook until the onions are nicely browned, about 30 minutes.

3. Sprinkle coarse cornmeal onto a pizza peel and place the dough on the peel. Using your hands, stretch the dough into a 14 x 16-inch rectangle, and brush with the oil. Season lightly with salt. Sprinkle the goat cheese, then the blueberries and onions, on the crust. Top with the rosemary, leaving a 1-inch border, and drizzle with honey.

4. Slide the pizza onto the baking stone and bake until the edge of the crust is slightly crisp and lightly browned, 20 to 25 minutes.

Knoll Farm

CONANT'S RIVERSIDE FARM/ RIVERSIDE PRODUCE

In 1854, Samuel Conant purchased Conant's Riverside Farm. At that time, the farm consisted of about 500 acres of cropland, forest, and pasture bordering the Winooski River. Today, the primary focus of the farm continues to be dairy. The sixth generation of Conant farmers now works on about 1,000 acres, which includes a combination of croplands and woodlands. They milk about 400 Holstein cows, and grow and sell sweet corn and other produce at their farmstand. They also market their own USDA-inspected ground beef during the produce season. The Conants are committed to continuing a tradition of sustainable environmental practices. Conant's Riverside Farm is a proud member of the Agri-Mark Dairy Co-operative, which supplies milk for such producers such as Cabot Creamery.

Fresh Corn Quiche

SERVES 6 TO 8

This light and creamy quiche is a nice departure from the traditional quiche with cheese.

3 large eggs, lightly beaten

½ small onion, coarsely chopped

1 tablespoon all-purpose flour

1 teaspoon kosher salt

½ teaspoon freshly ground black pepper

1⅓ cups half-and-half

3 tablespoons (1½ ounces) unsalted butter, melted

2 cups fresh corn kernels (cut from 2 to 3 ears corn) or frozen, thawed

1 tablespoon chopped fresh thyme or basil

1 (9-inch) prepared whole-wheat piecrust

1. Preheat the oven to 375°F.

2. Process the eggs, onion, flour, salt, and pepper in a food processor until the onion is finely chopped. Add the half-and-half and butter and process until just blended. Pour into a large bowl and stir in the corn and thyme. Pour the filling into the prepared crust.

3. Bake until the filling is slightly puffed and the top is golden brown, about 50 minutes. Remove from the oven and let cool slightly before serving.

Conant's Riverside Farm/Riverside Produce

JASPER HILL FARM

Brothers Andy and Mateo Kehler grew up summering on the edge of secluded Caspian Lake in the sleepy village of Greensboro. Their great grandfather had been a visitor to that area in the early 1900's. The brothers' long, emotional connection to the Northeast Kingdom made them decide to try to make a life there. When the opportunity arose in 1998, the two impulsively decided to buy a farm in Greensboro. They used the next three years to work on a business plan, gain the necessary experience to succeed as cheesemakers, and decide how best to use their farm's land.

Mateo spent two years in Europe working with farmstead cheesemakers in England, France, and Italy. After leaving Europe, he returned home. During the years 2002 to 2003, the brothers built a small cheese plant and began making cheese. Furthermore, the brothers began ripening cheeses for other cheesemakers in their storage area, known as the Cellars at Jasper Hill.

The Cellars at Jasper Hill was the first business of its kind in the United States. To achieve their goal, the brothers needed to blast out a hillside and pour monolithic concrete to create a structure that consists of seven vaulted tunnels, which are 22,000 square feet in size. These tunnels are nestled beneath the pastures where cows

graze. In that space, the Kehler's mature cheese for other cheesemakers.

Andy and Mateo are trying to assist dairy farmers who would like to transition from making commodity milk to the production of cheesemaking. By not having to make the investment in cheesemaking for their aging facilities, the dairy farmers increase the values of their farms. The Cellars at Jasper Hill offers the dairy farmer the labor to actually ripen the cheese. The brothers have a sales and marketing team to help the farm move their product. This frees the farmer from having to deal with the logistics necessary for getting the cheese to market and receiving payment. The Cellars at Jasper Hill basically take these tasks off the farmer's plate. This allows the producers to focus on the most important aspects of their trade—the quality milk production and cheesemaking techniques.

Part of the idea and inspiration for the Cellars at Jasper Hill evolved from Mateo's exposure to the cheese industry in England and France. What they are doing is an adaptation of what already exists in Europe, although their business is pretty different in some respects from anything that might exist in England or France.

The Kehler brothers have recently built an addition to their creamery and are now making a range of raw milk alpine cheeses. They have enlarged their milk producer pool, adding five local cow dairies from the communities of Greensboro, Craftsbury, and Glovers, as well as a goat farm in Hardwick. Jasper Hill Farm is all about offering consumers creatively produced, superior quality cheeses and supporting area farms and businesses.

Caramelized Onion and Bayley Hazen Blue Galette

SERVES 4 TO 6

This free-form tart is meant to have a rustic look, so don't worry if it is not perfect. The dough can be made up to one day ahead; just wrap and refrigerate. Bring the dough to room temperature before proceeding.

1¼ cups all-purpose flour

8 tablespoons (4 ounces) salted butter, cut into pieces and chilled

¼ cup crème fraîche

¼ cup ice water, plus extra as needed

2 tablespoons olive oil or bacon fat

4 medium yellow onions, peeled and thinly sliced

¹/₈ teaspoon granulated sugar

2 garlic cloves, minced

½ teaspoon finely chopped fresh rosemary or thyme

5 ounces blue cheese, preferably Bayley Hazen Blue Cheese, crumbled (1¼ cups)

1 large egg yolk, lightly beaten

1. Place the flour in a large bowl. Cut in the butter with a pastry cutter, two butter knives, or with your fingers, until the mixture begins to form pea-sized pieces. Combine the crème fraîche and ice water and add in a steady stream while mixing the dough with your fingertips. If necessary, add a bit more water until the dough holds together, but do not overmix. Turn the dough out onto a clean, floured work surface and form into a ball. Wrap in plastic wrap or waxed paper and refrigerate for at least 20 minutes.

2. Meanwhile, preheat the oven to 400°F. Heat the oil in a large skillet over medium heat. Add the onions and sugar and cook for 2 minutes. Reduce the heat to medium-low and continue to cook, stirring frequently, until the onions are soft and deeply browned, about 50 minutes, or depending on the size of the onion slices. Add the garlic and rosemary and cook for 1 minute.

3. On a floured work surface, roll the dough out into a 13-inch round. Transfer the dough to an ungreased baking sheet. Evenly spread the onion mixture over the dough, leaving a 1½-inch border. Evenly sprinkle the cheese over the top. Fold the border over the filling, pleating the edges as you go around. The center will be open. Brush the crust with the beaten egg yolk.

4. Bake the galette until the crust is golden brown and the cheese is sizzling, about 30 minutes. Remove from the oven and let cool for 5 minutes before cutting and serving.

Jasper Hill Farm

FLOWERPOWER VT

Anne Flack-Matthews' passion for farming began as a child. Her grandmother, an immigrant from Prussia, taught her how to garden and became her inspiration. Flack-Matthews grew up helping out in her family's vegetable garden and raising a lot of her own food. For her, the satisfaction of being outside and seeing things grow was magical.

The love of gardening was in her blood and continues to be a strong presence in her life. Throughout her younger years, Flack-Matthews somehow always managed to have a garden, beginning with 4H Club and continuing with a college community plot.

When she moved to a rural area in Pennsylvania, she bought 20 Araucana chickens at an Amish auction. This breed, native to Chile, lays eggs with light blue shells. Her three young children very much enjoyed taking care of the pear-shaped chickens with tufted "ears."

Ten years ago Flack-Matthews and her family moved to Vermont, where they bought a defunct llama farm, on a south-facing slope in Ferrisburgh. Flack-Matthews named the farm Flower-Power VT because it symbolized what the 1960s meant to her: peace, love, and understanding. Soon she bought a tiller and began planting flowering perennials, herbs, and vegetables. The farm's main focus was growing organic flowers, which were sold at various farmers' markets. Creating flower arrangements for weddings and local events also kept Flack-Matthews very busy. Still, she felt that something was missing: her beloved Araucana chickens.

Following her dream, she purchased 100 Araucana chicks. She sectioned off part of the farm to create a large area for the chicks to eat grass, bugs, and worms. Eventually, certified organic blue eggs were added to her onsite, year-round milk house farm stand and farmers, market offerings. Loyal customers couldn't get enough of the delicious dark golden yolks. FlowerPower VT has also added Americana chickens to their happy group.

Today, FlowerPower is a sustainable farm, utilizing all of their compost from their cut flower business. Their hens are also fed non-GMO feed grains from Green Mountain Feeds in Bethel, Vermont. If you're searching for FlowerPower products, you can find their bouquets sold at City Market, Onion River Co-op in Burlington. And they have even started farming the llamas and sheep for wool, with the yarn being available at Must Love Yarn in Shelburne.

Flack-Matthews says, "Never give up, follow your dreams and believe in yourself—that's me! My community is becoming what I envisioned. The interaction has been the most rewarding part, by far. I have muscles, sunburn, sore shoulders, and a smile."

Farm Quiche

SERVES 8

This quiche recipe showcases the farm's fresh, delicious Araucana eggs. The rich, creamy filling is studded with baby spinach, cherry tomatoes, and Gruyère cheese.

1½ tablespoons butter

⅔ cup chopped shallots (about 3 medium)

1½ cups packed chopped fresh baby spinach

Coarse salt and freshly ground white pepper

6 large eggs, beaten

1 cup whole milk

½ cup heavy cream

1½ teaspoons finely chopped fresh thyme

⅛ teaspoon grated nutmeg

1 (9-inch) whole-wheat pie crust, chilled

6 ounces Gruyère cheese, shredded (1½ cups)

8 cherry tomatoes, halved

1. Preheat the oven to 375°F.

2. Melt the butter in a large skillet over medium-low heat. Add the shallots and sauté until tender, 3 to 4 minutes. Add the spinach and cook until just wilted, 2 to 3 minutes. Season with salt and pepper to taste. When cool enough to handle, transfer the spinach mixture to a paper towel and squeeze out any excess water. Set aside.

3. Whisk together the eggs, milk, cream, thyme, nutmeg, and salt and pepper to taste.

4. Spread the spinach mixture evenly over the bottom of the pie crust. Sprinkle 1 cup of the Gruyère on top of the spinach and carefully pour the egg mixture over the cheese. Sprinkle with the remaining cheese and arrange the tomatoes over filling. Bake until the egg mixture is still slightly wiggly in center, about 40 minutes. Let cool for 15 minutes, then cut into wedges and serve.

FlowerPower VT

THISTLE HILL FARM

Thistle Hill Farm in North Pomfret, Vermont, is owned by John and Janine Putnam. The couple had "milked" for the past 26 years until they sold their dairy cows last April and the remainder of the Jerseys this past spring. The cows went to an Amish farm in Pennsylvania and, to the couples' relief, are doing well. Things change—as the cows are gone, so is milk production, which also means no cheese. The Putnam's have been cheesemakers for 20 years. The awards on their wall speak to how successful the farm was at one time.

Never folks to give up, John and Janine are now going into the beef business. They will be dealing with a rare breed of cattle called Randalls, which are indigenous to Vermont. The hardworking couple hope that this latest venture will soon be in every cook's repertoire and Thistle Hill Farm will have another award to add to its collection.

Tarentaise Bread Pudding

SERVES 12

Tarentaise cheese is smooth and dense, with a slightly nutty flavor and a natural rind.

4 tablespoons (2 ounces) unsalted butter

½ cup minced onion

2 garlic cloves, minced

1 tablespoon chopped fresh thyme

4 cups fresh whole-wheat bread crumbs

4 cups chicken stock

3 ounces Tarentaise cheese, shredded (¾ cup)

1 large egg plus 2 large egg yolks, lightly beaten

Kosher salt and freshly ground black pepper

1. Preheat the oven to 350°F. Coat twelve 6-ounce ramekins with nonstick cooking spray; set aside.

2. Melt the butter in a small skillet over medium heat. Add the onion and cook, stirring occasionally, until soft and translucent, about 5 minutes. Add the garlic and cook, stirring often for 1 minute. Stir in the thyme and set aside.

3. In a large bowl, stir together the onion mixture, bread crumbs, stock, cheese, egg and yolks, and salt and pepper to taste until fully combined.

4. Divide the mixture into the prepared ramekins. Place in a roasting pan, add enough hot water to come halfway up the sides of the ramekins and cover the pan with foil. Poke small holes in the foil to allow steam to release.

5. Bake 15 minutes, then carefully rotate the pan and bake an additional 15 minutes. Carefully remove the foil and bake until the puddings are golden brown, 10 minutes. Serve immediately.

Carpenter and Main Restaurant for Thistle Hill Farm

POORHOUSE PIES

When Jamie and Paula Eisenberg sold their pie business to longtime friend and restaurateur Suzanne Tomlinson in November 2021, both parties found themselves about to embark on a whole new chapter of their lives. Located in Underhill, Vermont, Poorhouse Pies specializes in making traditional and innovative sweet and savory pies, prepared in small batches. Continuing this tradition, its new owner has moved the business around the corner from the original pie shed into a building that once housed the town's post office.

For three months, Tomlinson trained with Eisenberg to learn the workings of the business and the technique of pie making. In the meantime, Tomlinson's contractor husband was busily building a bakery within the vacant post office. Much to everyone's delight, the task was completed in a mere 36 days. The building now has a rustic feel, very much like that of the original pie shed. However, the new kitchen is 10 times the size of its predecessor, allowing an opportunity to expand the variety and volume of the pies that are produced.

By using seasonal and local ingredients, the plan is to keep the pies as much like the original product as possible. For the most part, the assortment of pies remains the same—classics like maple cream and cherry are always in demand. Savory chicken pot and shepherd's pie, as well as pulled pork macaroni and cheese, keep folks coming back for more. Adventurous spirits will find that inventive pies are a fun way to put their own spin on a bakery creation. The line of customers that often stretch out the door is a visual testament to Poorhouse Pies' success. The long-range goal is to continue the winning traditions that were initiated by Eisenberg all those many years ago, this time with a focus on making "way more pie."

Along with savory pies, gluten-free and vegan options are now available. Although the concentration is primarily on the pie end of the business, donuts will also be offered from time to time. Tomlinson is very grateful for the community's enduring support. It is obvious to all that Poorhouse Pies has become a local treasure . . . as those who frequent the business like to say, "Pie Fixes Everything!"

Fiddlehead Quiche

**MAKES 1 (9-INCH) QUICHE;
SERVES 8**

Fiddleheads should never be eaten raw, always boil or steam before using in any recipe. This fern's furled frond is harvested in late April, May, and early June. If unavailable, fresh fiddleheads can be substituted for asparagus spears because their flavor and texture are similar.

Crust

1¼ cup all-purpose flour, plus extra for rolling

½ teaspoon salt

3 tablespoons unsalted butter, cut
    into small cubes chilled

1 tablespoon shortening

3 to 4 tablespoons ice-cold water

Fiddlehead Ferns

2 cups fiddleheads ferns, trimmed or
    asparagus spears (see Note)

Caramelized Onions

1 large yellow onion, peeled and thinly
    sliced into half-moons

⅛ teaspoon granulated sugar

1 tablespoon unsalted butter

⅛ teaspoon kosher salt

⅛ teaspoon freshly ground black pepper

Custard

5 large eggs, beaten

¾ cup heavy cream

⅓ cup whole milk

½ teaspoon minced garlic

½ teaspoon fresh minced thyme

½ teaspoon kosher salt

¼ teaspoon red pepper flakes

¼ teaspoon freshly ground black pepper

1¼ cups shredded aged cheddar cheese, divided

¼ cup shredded Swiss cheese

Garnish

Fresh minced parsley

1. To make the crust: Combine the flour and salt in a large bowl. With a pastry blender, cut the butter and shortening into the flour until just crumbly. Add the water, 1 tablespoon at a time, and mix until the dough just comes together. Turn the dough out onto a lightly floured surface and form into a disk. Wrap in plastic wrap, refrigerate, and let rest for 1½ hours.

2. On a lightly floured surface, roll the disk of dough out into a 12-inch round. Transfer to a 9-inch pie plate, trim the excess dough, leaving a ½-inch over-hang, and crimp the edges. Place the crust in the refrigerator and chill for at least 30 minutes.

3. To prepare the fiddleheads: Place a large bowl of ice water near your cooking area. Rinse the fiddle-heads well and set aside. Bring 6 cups of water to a boil over medium-high heat. Add the fiddleheads and boil for 10 minutes. Drain in a colander and plunge the fiddleheads into the ice-water bath for 2 minutes, then dry thoroughly with paper towels. Transfer to a bowl and set aside until ready to use.

4. To make the caramelized onions: Heat the but-ter in a medium skillet over medium heat. Add the onion and sugar and cook for 2 minutes. Reduce the heat to low and continue to cook, stirring frequently,

until the onions are soft and golden brown, about 40 minutes, depending on the size of the onion slices.

5. Preheat the oven to 350°F. Line a baking sheet with foil and set aside.

6. To make the filling: Whisk together the eggs, cream, milk, garlic, thyme, salt, red pepper flakes, and black pepper, until well combined.

7. Place the pie plate on the prepared baking sheet. Spread 1 cup of the cheddar cheese evenly over the bottom of the pie crust. Arrange the fiddleheads and caramelized onions evenly over the cheese. Carefully pour the egg mixture over the top. Sprinkle the remaining ¼ cup of cheddar cheese and the Swiss cheese over the filling. Bake until the egg mixture is barely wiggly in the center, about 40 to 45 minutes.

Transfer to a cooling rack and let rest for 15 minutes, then cut into wedges. Garnish with parsley and serve.

Note: If you are substituting asparagus for the fiddleheads use approximately 11 spears (about 9 ounces), cut into 1-inch sections. Place a large bowl of ice water near your cooking area. Bring 6 cups of water to a boil over medium-high heat. Add the asparagus spears and boil for about 5 to 7 minutes, depending on the thickness of the spears. Drain in a colander and plunge the spears into the ice water for 2 minutes, then dry thoroughly with paper towels. Transfer to a bowl and set aside until ready to use.

Poorhouse Pies

Brioche aux Champignons

SERVES 8

You will need to start the Brioche (page 24) at least two days before you intend to use it for the Brioche aux Champignons.

Brioche

8 (¾-inch) slices from one loaf Brioche (page 24)

Mushrooms

2 pounds local seasonal mushrooms, cleaned and quartered (about 12 cups)

½ teaspoon kosher salt, evenly divided

BHAKTA Crème Sauce

1 tablespoons extra virgin olive oil

1 small shallot finely diced, about ¼ cup, divided

5 large fresh sage leaves, cut into slivers

2 tablespoons brandy

½ cup heavy cream, room temperature

¼ teaspoon kosher salt

¼ teaspoon freshly ground black pepper

Spinach

1 tablespoon extra-virgin olive oil

1 pound organic spinach, cleaned and stemmed (just under 1 gallon of leaves, loosely packed)

¼ teaspoon kosher salt

¼ teaspoon freshly ground black pepper

14 ounces Comté cheese, cut into thin slices

1. Position an oven rack one notch down from directly underneath the broiler. Line a broiler proof baking sheet with foil. Arrange the brioche slices in a single layer on the prepared baking sheet. Set aside.

2. To make the mushrooms: Heat a dry, carbon steel fry pan over medium heat. Add the mushrooms in batches, being careful not to overcrowd. Dry-sauté the mushrooms until they become fragrant and turn a nice golden brown, about 8 minutes. Sprinkle with ½ teaspoon salt and toss until evenly coated then transfer to a bowl. Repeat with the remaining mushrooms and salt.

3. To make the brandy cream sauce: Heat 1 tablespoon of olive oil in a small sauté pan over medium heat. Add half of the diced shallots and the sage leaves, then sauté for about 1 minute. Do not burn the sage. Remove the pan from the stovetop and carefully add the brandy. Return the pan to the heat and bring the liquid to a simmer. Deglaze the pan, stirring frequently, scraping the bits from the bottom. In a slow and steady stream, whisk in the heavy cream. Season with the ¼ teaspoon salt and ¼ teaspoon pepper, then reduce the heat to a bare simmer, stirring occasionally until you are ready to use the cream sauce.

4. For the spinach: Using the same skillet as the mushrooms, heat 1 tablespoon of the olive oil over medium heat. Add the remaining shallots and sauté for 1 minute. Add the spinach and sauté until the spinach has wilted, about 5 minutes. Season with ¼ teaspoon salt and ¼ teaspoon pepper.

5. Preheat the oven broiler to high.

6 To prepare the toasted brioche: Transfer the prepared baking sheet with the brioche slices to the broiler and toast one side until golden brown, about 1 minute. Remove baking sheet from broiler. Using tongs, flip the bread slices over, and cover each with cheese slices, draping some of the slices over the edges of the bread. Transfer back to the broiler and toast until the bread slices are golden brown and the cheese has melted, about 1 minute. During broiling, it is important to keep a close eye on the brioche to avoid burning.

7. To assemble: Combine the spinach and any remaining liquid with the mushrooms, tossing until well combined. Place the cheese toasts on individual plates, top with the sautéed spinach-mushroom mixture. Spoon 1 tablespoon of the BHAKTA Crème Sauce over the top of each brioche toast. Adjust seasonings with salt if desired. Serve at once.

Note: If you can't find Comte cheese, the best substitute is Swiss Gruyère because it is similar in both texture and taste.

Chef Philip Davis for BHAKTA 50 Spirits

PASTA AND POLENTA

Stone-Ground Cheese Grits with Wild Foraged Mushrooms

**MAKES 4 SERVINGS;
MAKES 4¼ CUPS GRITS**

"I like to use Invierno (means winter in Spanish) cheese for this dish. Vermont Shepherd, located in Westminster, Vermont, makes this local mixed milk cheese from sheep's milk and organic cow's milk. If you don't have access to this versatile cheese, feel free to use a Parmigiano-Reggiano or Grandano Vecchio cheese," says owner Michael Fuller.

Wild Foraged Mushrooms

½ pound local seasonal mushrooms, cleaned and quartered (about 4 cups)

¼ teaspoon kosher salt

Grits

3½ cups water

½ cup dry white wine

1 cup of stone-ground heirloom white corn grits, medium cut

¾ teaspoon salt, or to taste

½ cup shredded cheese, such as Invierno, Parmigiano-Reggiano, or Grandano Vecchio

¼ cup heavy cream, warmed

¼ teaspoon freshly ground black pepper, or to taste

3 tablespoons extra-virgin olive oil

½ cup lightly packed microgreens for garnish

1. To make the mushrooms: Heat a dry, carbon steel fry pan over medium heat. Add the mushrooms, being careful not to overcrowd. Dry-sauté the mushrooms until they become fragrant and turn a nice golden brown, about 8 minutes. Sprinkle with salt and toss until evenly coated then transfer to a bowl until ready to use.

2. To make the grits: Add the water and wine to a 2-quart saucepan and bring to a boil over medium-high heat, about 7 minutes. Add the grits in a slow and steady stream, stirring frequently with a wooden spoon. Reduce the heat to low, then add the salt and continue to cook, stirring frequently until the grits are tender and thicken, about 8 to 12 minutes, or depending on the grind.

3. Remove from the heat, then fold in the cheese, heavy cream, and black pepper. Add the olive oil 1 tablespoon at a time, until well combined. Adjust seasonings with additional salt and pepper, if desired.

4. To serve: Divide the grits among four bowls, about 1 cup per serving. Evenly scatter the mushrooms over the top then garnish with microgreens. Serve at once.

T.J. Buckley's Uptown Dining

T.J. BUCKLEY'S UPTOWN DINING

The saying "Good things come in small packages" is the perfect way to describe T.J. Buckley's Uptown Dining establishment, which is located in Brattleboro, Vermont. The quaint restaurant is tucked inside of a restored 1925 Worcester Dining Car that lends a unique ambience to each occasion. While small in size, the charming eight-table restaurant imparts a feeling of elegance to the evening's festivities.

The dining car's open kitchen offers guests an opportunity to observe chef and owner, Michael Fuller, skillfully prepare his exquisite selection of culinary masterpieces. Chef Fuller has been cooking with unusual ingredients for more than three decades. His French culinary background has trained him to prepare dishes with a simple, elegant flair.

As a result of the restaurant's ingredient-driven menu, the chef has developed a strong connection with the area's produce growers. Chef Buckley has lived the farm-to-table way of life from a very early age, strongly believing in and supporting the idea of knowing where your food comes from. He likes to integrate wild edibles into his cuisine, often building his menu around what he collects when exploring the countryside. Some of his favorites are ramps, morel, maitake, and black trumpet, as well as other selections that may be in season. The busy chef feels that good food is well worth the effort. This philosophy trickles down to food choices, exemplified by the fish that he uses, which must be caught by using sustainable fishing practices.

Instead of a printed menu, guests will be informed of the evening's offerings by their very knowledgeable server. The selection of dishes usually includes three appetizers, four entrées, and four desserts that are updated weekly. The menu varies seasonally and is contingent upon the availability of local ingredients. Vegetarian, gluten-free, and vegan selections are always on-hand, as are meat, poultry, and fish.

T.J. Buckley's Uptown Dining offers a wonderful collection of wine and beer that have been selected by its owner. Handpicked to go with each evening's menu, the white or red wine, dessert wine, and champagne are all geared to complement specific dishes. From the start of the sumptuous meal with its exquisite presentation to the final delicious forkful of dessert, Chef Fuller strives to make each dinner deliciously unique, creating a fond memory that lingers long after the day ends.

Penne with Creamy Smugglers' Notch Vodka Sauce

SERVES 4 TO 6

Penne pasta with vodka sauce (penne alla vodka) is a classic that is fun to bring out now and again. This dish is smooth and lightly creamy, with a hint of sweetness from the Smugglers' Notch vodka and a slight nuttiness from the freshly grated Parmigiano-Reggiano cheese. The key to this dish is using very fresh ingredients, from the spinach to the shrimp and scallops, making sure not to overcook the seafood. To prevent a flare-up, be sure to remove the skillet from the heat before adding the vodka.

Kosher salt and freshly ground black pepper

1 pound whole-wheat penne

3 tablespoons olive oil

1 pound jumbo shrimp (16/20 count), peeled and deveined

12 ounces sea scallops (20/30 count), tendons removed

8 slices prosciutto, coarsely chopped

2 tablespoons minced shallot

2 garlic cloves, minced

3 plum tomatoes, seeded and cut into thin strips

3 cups baby spinach

⅓ cup Smugglers' Notch vodka

1¼ cups natural marinara sauce

1 cup heavy cream

2 ounces Parmigiano-Reggiano or Pecorino Romano cheese, grated (1 cup), plus extra for serving

2 tablespoons chopped fresh basil

1. Bring a large pot of salted water to a boil, add the pasta, and cook until al dente, 6 to 7 minutes. Drain in a colander and set aside.

2. Meanwhile, heat the oil in a large skillet over medium-high heat. Add the shrimp and scallops and cook, 1 to 2 minutes on each side. Season with salt and pepper to taste. Add the prosciutto and continue to cook until the scallops are caramelized, about 2 minutes.

3. Reduce the heat to medium, add the shallot, garlic, tomatoes, and spinach, and cook for 1 minute. Remove the skillet from the heat and carefully add the vodka. Return to heat and cook until the alcohol burns off, about 2 minutes. Add the marinara sauce and heavy cream and simmer for 2 minutes. Stir in ½ cup of the cheese until melted and smooth. Add the pasta to the sauce and cook until heated through. Season with salt and pepper to taste.

4. Transfer the pasta to a large bowl and sprinkle with the remaining ½ cup cheese, tossing to incorporate. Sprinkle with the basil and serve with additional cheese.

Chef Peter McLyman for Smugglers' Notch Distillery

HERMIT'S GOLD WILD EDIBLES

At a very young age, Colin McCaffrey began foraging for wild edibles in the Connecticut River Valley of Vermont. His mother showed him how to cook milkweed shoots and roast dandelion roots, as well as harvest wild berries, nettles, and fiddleheads. His first taste of wild mushrooms was freshly picked inky caps sautéed in butter. McCaffrey spent hours in the woods hunting, fishing, and learning the names of wildflowers and the properties of herbs. After settling in central Vermont, he has spent the past three decades learning the woods around his home and beyond, seeking out the best edible plants and fungi. His "day job" is record producer, songwriter, and musician.

Spaghetti and Porcini Mushroom Meatballs

SERVES 4

This recipe is one of McCaffrey's favorite ways of using the porcini and *Boletus edulis* mushrooms that he harvests and dries all summer. The intense, earthy flavor of the dried porcini mushroom is a wonderful compliment to grass-fed beef. Colin has made these meatballs with a brown gravy served on mashed potatoes as well as in a tomato sauce with pasta. Each approach brings out different subtleties of spice and mushroom flavor.

½ ounce dried porcini mushrooms, not rehydrated

1 teaspoon paprika

1 teaspoon ground cumin

½ teaspoon salt

½ teaspoon freshly ground black pepper

¼ teaspoon grated nutmeg

⅛ teaspoon curry powder

1 pound ground beef, preferably grass-fed

½ cup finely ground bread crumbs or panko

¼ cup finely grated Parmigiano-Reggiano
   cheese, plus extra for serving

1 large egg, lightly beaten

1 large garlic clove, minced

2 tablespoons olive oil

3 cups good-quality tomato-basil pasta sauce

12 ounces whole-wheat spaghetti

1. Pulse the mushrooms, paprika, cumin, salt, pepper, nutmeg, and curry powder in a food processor until well combined.

2. In a large bowl mix the mushroom-spice mixture, beef, bread crumbs, Parmigiano-Reggiano, egg, and garlic until just combined. Using your hands, form into approximately 16 meatballs, depending on how large the meatballs are rolled.

3. Heat 1 tablespoon of the oil in a large skillet over medium-high heat. Add half of the meatballs and cook, turning until browned on all sides, about 7 minutes. With a slotted spoon, transfer the meatballs to a plate. Repeat with the remaining oil and remaining meatballs. Return all the meatballs to the skillet. Add the pasta sauce and simmer until the meatballs have reached an internal temperature of 140°F, about 15 minutes.

4. Meanwhile, bring a large pot of salted water to a boil over medium-high heat. Add the pasta and cook according to the package directions until al dente. Drain in a colander. Place the pasta in a large bowl and top with the meatballs and sauce. Serve with additional grated Parmigiano-Reggiano cheese, if desired.

Hermit's Gold Wild Edibles

Alpen Macaroni

SERVES 8 TO 10

Tarentaise cheese is smooth-textured, subtly nut-flavored and naturally rinded. Serve this rich dish with a green salad and a nice crusty baguette.

1 pound macaroni

2 medium potatoes, unpeeled,
    cut into ¼-inch cubes

8 ounces (about 8 slices) bacon

1 large onion, chopped

3 garlic cloves, minced

2 tablespoons (1 ounce) unsalted butter

2 tablespoons all-purpose flour

6 ounces Tarentaise cheese, shredded (1½ cups)

1–1½ cups light cream

2 teaspoons dry mustard

Kosher salt and freshly ground black pepper

Cayenne pepper

Chopped fresh thyme or parsley, for garnish

1. Preheat the oven to 350°F. Lightly grease a 10 x 15-inch baking dish with butter or coat with nonstick cooking spray; set aside. Bring a large pot of salted water to a boil over medium-high heat. Add the macaroni and cook according to the package directions until al dente. Drain in a colander and set aside.

2. Place the potatoes in a medium saucepan and cover with cold, salted water. Bring to a boil over medium-high heat and cook until the potatoes are just tender. Drain in a colander and set aside.

3. Cook the bacon in a medium skillet over medium-high heat until crisp, 5 to 6 minutes. Let the bacon drain on paper towels, then coarsely chop it. Pour off all but 2 tablespoons of the bacon fat from the skillet, then add the onion and cook over medium-high heat, stirring occasionally, until soft and translucent, about 5 minutes. Add the garlic and cook, stirring occasionally, for 1 minute.

4. Melt the butter in a medium saucepan over medium-low heat. Whisk in the flour and cook until the mixture has thickened and the flour is a pale golden color. Remove from the heat and stir in the bacon, 1 cup of the cheese, the cream, and dry mustard. Season with salt and pepper to taste.

5. In a large bowl, stir together the macaroni, potatoes, and the cheese mixture until well combined then transfer to the prepared baking dish. Lightly coat the dull side of a sheet of foil with nonstick cooking spray and cover the baking dish.

6. Bake the macaroni and cheese until hot and bubbly, about 20 minutes. Remove the dish from the oven and sprinkle the remaining ½ cup cheese and cayenne pepper to taste over the top. Return to the oven and bake, uncovered, until the cheese is golden brown, about 10 minutes. Let rest for 10 minutes, sprinkle with thyme, and serve.

Thistle Hill Farm

Pasta with Goat Cheese and Roasted Tomatoes

SERVES 4 TO 6

Blue Ledge Farm was established in the year 2000. It is a family-owned and -operated goat dairy farm and farmstead cheese operation. Their mission is to create a high-quality product built on the cornerstones of respect for the consumer, land, and animals, as well as the local community. This soft-textured pasta dish is creamy, fresh, and aromatic, with a nice lingering tanginess from the goat cheese. The plump, juicy Kalamata olives give it a meat-like taste. Substitute whole-wheat penne pasta for added protein and fiber if you prefer. Just be sure make sure to cook the pasta al dente because it will cook more when the starchy pasta water is incorporated.

2½ pounds cherry tomatoes, halved,
      or whole grape tomatoes

2 tablespoons olive oil

Salt and freshly ground black pepper

1 pound penne

6 ounces fresh goat cheese, crumbled (1½ cups)

½ cup pitted Kalamata olives, halved

¾ cup chopped fresh basil, plus extra for garnish

2 teaspoons fresh lemon juice

⅓ cup grated Parmesan cheese

1. Preheat the oven to 425°F.

2. Place the tomatoes on a baking sheet, drizzle with olive oil, and season with salt and pepper to taste. Roast for 15 minutes and set aside.

3. Bring 6 quarts of salted water to a boil in a large pot over medium-high heat. Add the pasta and cook just until al dente. Drain the pasta, reserving ⅔ cup of the pasta water.

4. While the pasta is cooking, combine the tomatoes, goat cheese, olives, basil, and lemon juice in a large bowl. Add the hot pasta and toss, mixing well. Slowly add the reserved pasta water as needed, stirring until the sauce is creamy. Season with salt and pepper to taste.

5. To serve, spoon pasta into warm bowls and top with Parmesan. Garnish with basil and serve at once.

Blue Ledge Farm

BUTTERWORKS FARM

Butterworks Farm, located in Westfield, is one of New England's first certified organic dairy farms. Started in 1976 with a few Jersey cows and homestead on 60 acres, the farm now cares for a herd of 70 Jerseys (all are born on the farm and given names) and about 350 acres of grassland. The Butterworks team packs and ships about 7,500 pounds of yogurt, buttermilk, kefir, and heavy cream from its on-farm processing facility each week.

The Lazor family has always been committed to soil health. Farming practices that promote biodiversity, restore nutrients, and build soil carbon through slow-aged composting, no-till seeding, and rotational grazing. In 2016, Butterworks transitioned the herd to 100-percent grass-fed and continues to operate as an all-grass farm.

Jack Lazor passed away in 2020. He was well-known for his passion for ecological agriculture and innovative farming practices. As a three-generation family farm, Butterworks faces new challenges each year and strives to remain responsive and adaptable to the climate environment, market, and community.

POULTRY

THE GLEANERY

In 2013, Ismail Samad opened his restaurant, The Gleanery, in Putney, Vermont. Samad, believing that reducing food waste is the most approachable way to make our kitchens more sustainable, practices this philosophy at his restaurant. The Gleanery Restaurant eliminates waste and showcases culinary artistry with high-end farm products. This practice provides economic opportunities for local farm partners. The Gleanery is a farm-first, closed-loop restaurant, meaning that little to no waste is created from gathering, preparing, or cooking its food. The chef/food advocate emphasizes that using an ingredient in its entirety is economical and part of the art of cooking.

Samad's dedication to innovative food approaches is grounded by his desire to establish new standards for creative food ventures that are driven by equity, sustainability, and collaboration. This is guided by a respect for the environment. To achieve these goals the chef has cofounded the nonprofit Loiter, where he does consulting on zero-waste strategies and other related projects.

Roasted Pheasant with Thyme-Roasted Sweet Potatoes and Sherry Cream

SERVES 2 TO 4

Ismail Samad, executive chef at the Gleanery, in Putney, welcomes the challenge of creating dishes around what is available locally. Creativity plays a crucial role in the way Chef Ismail prepares each recipe and is what makes his job fun and rewarding. The recipe concept for this dish started with a conversation with a farmer who raised fowl and rabbits. If you can't find pheasant, you can substitute quail or chicken. See photo on page 117.

Sweet Potatoes and Pheasant

2 large (about 1½ pounds) sweet potatoes, peeled and cut into 1-inch pieces

1 large sweet onion, cut into 1-inch pieces

5 tablespoons olive oil

4 tablespoons (2 ounces) unsalted butter, melted

8 sprigs fresh thyme

Kosher salt and freshly ground black pepper

1 (2- to 3-pound) pheasant, cut into 4 pieces and trimmed

Sherry Cream

⅓ cup dry sherry

1 shallot, sliced thin

2 teaspoons chopped fresh thyme, plus extra for garnish

Pinch red pepper flakes

1 cup heavy cream

Kosher salt and freshly ground black pepper

1. To make the sweet potatoes and pheasant: Preheat the oven to 350°F. Combine the sweet potatoes, onion, 2 tablespoons of the oil, 2 tablespoons of the butter, 4 sprigs of the thyme, and salt and pepper to taste in a large bowl, tossing to coat. Transfer to a baking dish and bake until the sweet potatoes are tender, about 40 minutes.

2. Increase the oven temperature to 400°F. Season the pheasant with salt and pepper to taste. Heat the remaining 3 tablespoons of oil in a large skillet over medium-high heat until hot, but not smoking. Add the pheasant, skin side down, and sear for 2 to 3 minutes. Add the remaining 2 tablespoons of butter and remaining 4 sprigs thyme, transfer the skillet to the oven and cook the pheasant for about 25 minutes, flipping the pieces over halfway through the cooking time.

3. To make the sherry cream: While the pheasant is cooking, combine the sherry, shallot, thyme, and pepper flakes in a medium saucepan over low heat and simmer until the sauce is reduced by half. Slowly whisk in the cream and cook until the mixture is reduced by one-third. Season with salt and pepper to taste. Pour the mixture through a fine-mesh strainer and cover to keep warm.

4. Transfer the sweet potatoes to a microwave-safe bowl and microwave until hot. Divide the sweet potatoes and pheasant among four plates, spoon the sherry cream over the pheasant, sprinkle with chopped thyme, and serve.

Chef Ismail Samad of the Gleanery

MISTY KNOLL FARMS

Misty Knoll Farms is a family-owned and operated farm, producing the finest naturally raised turkeys and chickens available in Vermont.

As stewards of Vermont's working landscape owners John Palmer and Rob Litch treat their farm as a precious, irreplaceable resource, following sustainable farming practices to ensure that their cropland will be productive for future generations. The two raise their birds with the utmost care, feeding them whole grains, free of antibiotics and animal by-products. Their chickens roam in spacious, specially designed enclosures. The result—healthy, nutritious, and flavorful birds, nature's way.

By processing the turkeys and chickens on-site, in their own USDA-inspected facility, they subject the birds to minimal stress. Palmer and Litch carefully grade them by hand to assure that only the finest birds are available for sale.

Chicken Paprika

SERVES 4

Eric Seitz, co-owner of Pitchfork Farm, got this hearty, earthy recipe from his Hungarian grand-mother. Serve with Hungarian Nokedli (page 21).

**8 bone-in, skin-on chicken thighs, legs,
  or split breasts, trimmed**

Kosher salt and freshly ground black pepper

Garlic powder

2 tablespoons olive oil

1 large sweet onion, thinly sliced

**1 green bell pepper, stemmed,
  seeded and thinly sliced**

**1 red bell pepper, stemmed,
  seeded and thinly sliced**

2½ cups low-sodium chicken broth

2 tablespoons sweet Hungarian paprika

1 large tomato, seeded and chopped

½ cup sour cream

1 tablespoon all-purpose flour

Chopped fresh parsley

1. Season the chicken with salt, pepper, and garlic powder to taste. Heat the oil in a large skillet over medium-high heat. Working in batches, add half of the chicken pieces and brown, about 3 minutes per side, then transfer to a platter. Repeat with the remaining chicken.

2. Using the same skillet for browning the chicken, add the onions and bell peppers. Reduce the heat to medium and cook, stirring often until the onions are soft and translucent. You may need to add a little oil to the pan. Return the chicken back to the skillet with the onions and peppers. Stir in the broth and paprika and bring to a simmer. Cover and cook until the chicken has cooked through, about 30 minutes.

3. Remove the chicken from the skillet and stir in the tomatoes. Whisk together the sour cream and flour and stir into the sauce; cook until heated through. Season with salt to taste, sprinkle with parsley, and serve.

Pitchfork Farm

CLOUDLAND FARM

Cloudland Farm was originally a 2,000-acre dairy farm when Bill Emmons's grandfather and great grandfather purchased the property in the early 1900s. Today, the diversified family-run farm consists of just over 1,000 acres, 4 miles from the town of Woodstock. The current owners, Bill and his wife, Cathy, raise Black Angus beef cattle, pastured chickens and turkeys, pigs, and vegetables, as well as running a certified tree farm and the Cloudland Farm Country Market.

Raising happy, healthy animals and producing wholesome food is very important to the Emmons family. The owners of Cloudland Farm pride themselves on being good stewards of the land, while producing the most nutritious feed for their animals. The farm uses no growth hormones or antibiotics, except in rare cases of life-threatening illness. All of their animals are pastured. During the winter months, the animals feed on hay that is produced on the farm, without the use of chemical fertilizers.

Cloudland Farm also offers an on-farm restaurant, which is open for dinner on Thursday, Friday, and Saturday nights. The restaurant utilizes local food, most of which is organic. All of the meat served comes from the farm, as does a portion of the produce. The menu is limited to one prix fixe meal, selected and prepared by the chef, Mike Borraccio. With advance notice, Borraccio happily accommodates dietary restrictions or vegetarian preferences.

Chicken Breasts Stuffed with Chèvre and Sautéed Ramps Served with Pickled Ramps and Rhubarb Gastrique

SERVES 4

When ramps are no longer available, you can substitute a combination of 18 wild scallions and 6 garlic bulbs (small fresh heads of garlic with stalks). Reserve two garlic bulbs, including the lower end of the stalks, and 8 scallions for pickling. Chef Borraccio uses Vermont Butter and Cheese Creamery goat cheese in this dish. Serve with wild rice or pilaf, if desired.

Rhubarb Gastrique

1 cup granulated sugar

½ cup red wine vinegar

½ cup water

3 cups finely chopped rhubarb

1 teaspoon chopped fresh sage

Kosher salt and freshly ground black pepper

Sautéed Ramps

12–14 ramps, cleaned, green leaves discarded

4 tablespoons unsalted butter

Kosher salt and freshly ground black pepper

Chicken

4 (6-ounce) boneless, skin-on split chicken breasts, trimmed

8 ounces goat cheese

Kosher salt and freshly ground black pepper, to taste

3 tablespoons canola oil

Pickled Ramps (recipe follows)

1. Preheat the oven to 400°F. Lightly grease a baking sheet and set aside.

2. To make the rhubarb gastrique: Bring the sugar, vinegar, and water to a boil in a medium nonreactive saucepan. Add the rhubarb and sage and boil until the rhubarb is soft and the mixture has thickened, 5 to 10 minutes. Let cool for 10 to 15 minutes, then transfer to a blender or food processor and process until smooth. Season with salt and pepper to taste, spoon into a bowl, and set aside.

3. To make the sautéed ramps: Slice the bulbs and stalks into small rounds and slice the leaves into narrow strips. Melt the butter in a medium skillet over medium heat, add the bulbs and stalks and sauté until soft and tender. Add the leaves and cook until just wilted. Season with salt and pepper to taste. Let cool completely.

4. To make the chicken: Using a small sharp knife, cut horizontally through the center of each chicken breast, to within 1 inch of opposite side, creating a pocket. Spoon one-quarter of the sautéed ramps and one-quarter of the goat cheese into the pocket of each chicken breast. Season each chicken breast liberally with salt and pepper to taste.

5. Heat the oil in a large skillet over medium-high heat. Add the breasts and brown on both sides, about 4 minutes per side. Transfer the breasts to the prepared baking sheet, skin side up and bake for 20 to 25 minutes. Let rest for 5 minutes. Top with the rhubarb gastrique and pickled ramps and serve.

Cloudland Farm

PICKLED RAMPS

8–10 ramps, cleaned, green leaves discarded

⅓ cup water

⅓ cup white wine

⅓ cup white wine vinegar

⅓ cup granulated sugar

2 teaspoons salt

Place the ramp bulbs in a 16-ounce glass jar with a tight lid. Combine the water, wine, vinegar, sugar, and salt in a saucepan and bring to a boil over medium-high heat. Cook, stirring frequently, until the sugar is dissolved. Pour over the ramps and seal jar. Let cool to room temperature, then refrigerate for at least 3 hours.

Nick Mahood, former chef of Cloudland Farm

Cranberry and Turkey Sausage Stuffing

SERVES 12 TO 16

As with any stuffing recipe, the ingredients and flavor possibilities are endless—feel free to experiment. This recipe makes enough stuffing to fill an 18- to 20-pound turkey, with some extra stuffing left over. After stuffing the turkey (loosely, as the stuffing will expand when cooked), spoon the extra stuffing into a lightly buttered 8-inch square pan, dot with 1 tablespoon butter, and bake as directed.

1 (15-ounce) package all-purpose
    seasoned bread stuffing mix

6 tablespoons (3 ounces) unsalted butter

2 cups finely chopped yellow onions
    (about 2 small onions)

2 cups finely chopped celery (about 4 ribs)

1 Granny Smith apple, cored and chopped

2 garlic cloves, minced

2 teaspoons chopped fresh sage

2 teaspoons chopped fresh rosemary

1 teaspoon salt

1 tablespoon olive oil

1 pound mild turkey sausage, casings removed

1 cup mashed jellied cranberry sauce

1 cup Vermont apple cider, plus extra as needed

2 large eggs, lightly beaten

1. Preheat the oven to 350°F. Lightly butter a 9 x 13-inch baking dish and set aside. Place the bread stuffing mix in a very large bowl.

2. Melt 4 tablespoons of the butter in a large skillet over medium heat. Add the onions, celery, and apple and cook, stirring often, until the vegetables are soft and translucent, about 10 minutes. Stir in the garlic, sage, rosemary, and salt and cook for 1 minute. Add the vegetable mixture to the bread stuffing.

3. In the same skillet, heat the oil over medium heat. Add the sausage and cook, crumbling with a fork, until browned, about 7 minutes. Using a slotted spoon, transfer to the bowl with the bread stuffing.

4. Add the cranberry sauce, cider, and eggs to the bread stuffing. Gently mix all the ingredients together; do not overmix. Season with salt and pepper to taste. If the mixture seems too dry, add more cider until the desired consistency is reached.

5. Spoon the stuffing into the prepared baking dish. Cut the remaining 2 tablespoons of butter into small pieces and distribute them evenly over the stuffing. Cover with foil and bake for 25 minutes. Uncover and bake until golden brown on top, about 10 minutes. Serve.

Stonewood Farm

STONEWOOD FARM

Stonewood Farm is located in Orwell, on Vermont's western border. It is one of the largest turkey farms in New England, raising about 35,000 birds a year. The farm has been in the Stone family for generations, and they take great pride in raising all-natural turkeys that are free of hormones and antibiotics. Their birds are not caged but are housed in open-air barns, an arrangement that offers them lots of natural sunlight and fresh air, while protecting them from predators and disease. The farm's mission is to provide the people of Vermont and its surrounding states with quality turkeys that are humanely raised.

Green Chicken

SERVES 4

In this dish, you may use any type of fresh herb—or a combination of herbs—with delicious results, so try whatever you have and enjoy the green!

1 cup loosely packed fresh herbs, such as basil, Thai basil, cilantro, or mint

¼ cup extra-virgin olive oil

1 teaspoon grated lemon zest plus ¼ cup juice (2 lemons)

2 garlic cloves or 2 garlic scapes, coarsely chopped

Kosher salt and freshly ground black pepper

4 (6-ounce) boneless, skinless chicken breasts, trimmed and cut into 1-inch strips

1. Combine the herbs, oil, lemon zest and juice, garlic, and salt and pepper to taste in a food processor or blender and purée until a smooth paste forms.

2. Place the chicken strips in a large zip-top bag, add the herb paste, and stir to coat. Seal the bag and refrigerate for at least 30 minutes or up to 12 hours. Remove the chicken from the refrigerator 30 minutes before grilling.

3. Preheat a gas or electric grill to medium heat. Clean the grill grate and brush with oil. Place the chicken on the grill, cover, and cook, until cooked through, about 4 minutes per side.

Note: For an alternate method of preparation, put the raw marinated chicken and your favorite veggies on skewers to create flavorful kabobs. You may also spread the herb paste underneath the skin of a whole chicken before roasting it in the oven.

Sterling College

Roasted Chicken with Chilled Heirloom Tomato Purée and Scallion Rice Cakes Topped with Crispy Kale

SERVES 4

Black Krim tomatoes are really the best for this dish, given their low acidity and high sugar. They ripen so nicely during the summer months and create an amazing chilled purée. Other good choices include Paul Robeson, Moskovich, or Mountain Princess. This recipe has a wide variation of textures and flavors, from the crispy, salty kale, and light but substantial rice cakes to the juicy, savory chicken and the sweet, acidic tomato purée.

1 cup sushi rice

2 teaspoons seasoned rice vinegar

¼ cup chopped scallions

1 (3½-pound) whole chicken, giblets discarded

9 tablespoons olive oil

Kosher salt and freshly ground black pepper

6 medium heirloom tomatoes

4 garlic cloves, minced

1 teaspoon red pepper flakes, plus extra to taste

¼ cup chopped fresh cilantro

2 tablespoons red wine vinegar

1 bunch kale, stemmed and chopped

3 tablespoons vegetable oil

1. Preheat the oven to 375°F. Place the rice in a medium saucepan, add 1 cup water and bring to a simmer over medium heat. Cover lightly, reduce the heat to low and cook until tender, 30 to 35 minutes. Stir in the seasoned rice vinegar, let cool slightly, then stir in the scallions. Let cool completely.

2. Rinse the chicken and pat dry with paper towels. Rub with 3 tablespoons of the olive oil and season generously inside and out with salt and pepper. Place breast side up in a roasting pan. Roast the chicken, basting every 15 minutes, until the skin is golden brown, the juices run clear, and the chicken breast reaches an internal temperature of 160°F, about 1¼ hours. When the chicken is cool enough to handle, using two forks or your fingertips, shred or pull the meat from the bones and set aside.

3. Meanwhile, score the tomatoes and lay on a lined baking sheet. Sprinkle with 1 tablespoon olive oil and salt to taste and roast for 45 minutes or until the tomatoes are shriveled but tender. Let cool.

4. To make the garlic and chili oil: While the tomatoes and chicken are cooking, gently heat 4 tablespoons olive oil in a small saucepan over medium heat. Add the garlic and red pepper flakes and cook until the garlic is fragrant, but not colored, 2 to 3 minutes. Let the oil cool to room temperature.

5. When the tomatoes are cool enough to handle, place them in a blender, add the cilantro, garlic and chili oil, vinegar, and 1 teaspoon salt and purée until smooth. Season with salt and additional red pepper flakes, if desired. Transfer to a bowl, cover and refrigerate.

6. Place the kale in large skillet with ¼ cup water and cook over medium-high heat until the water has evaporated. Add the remaining 1 tablespoon olive oil and a pinch salt. Toss and lay on a parchment-lined baking sheet. Sprinkle with salt and roast in the oven for 30 minutes, or until dark green and crispy.

7. While the kale is roasting, wet your hands with warm water and, using a 2-ounce ice cream scoop, take one scoop of rice and form into a disk. Repeat with the remaining rice to make 4 disks. Heat the vegetable oil in a large skillet over medium-high heat. Add the rice cakes and cook until the edges start to brown, about 3 minutes per side.

8. Ladle ¼ cup of the tomato purée in an even circle on each plate. Place a rice cake in the center of the purée, then place some of the shredded chicken on top of the rice cake. Top with crispy kale and serve.

Pebble Brook Farm

PRESTON'S RESTAURANT AT KILLINGTON RESORT

Preston's Restaurant is located at the Grand Resort Hotel in the picturesque town of Killington, Vermont. The farm-to-table eatery is named after Preston L. Smith, the founder of this popular ski resort. Executive Chef Gregory J. Lang oversees the resort's kitchen, creating a menu that focuses on the area's farms and artisanal food producers. Culinary selections are reflective of this mountain community's "best of the best:" the farmers, cheesemakers, and brewers who are dedicated to raising and producing the finest regional ingredients and products possible.

Preston's Pure Honey-Glazed Chicken with Sweet Corn Spoonbread and Vanilla-Truffle Butter Sauce

SERVES 4

Timing and preparation are key for this recipe. It is important to have all of the ingredients prepped and measured out in advance because there's not much time between the steps to do measuring or prepping.

Sweet Corn Spoonbread

2 large ears of corn with husks on

½ tablespoon unsalted butter, or as need for greasing skillet

½ cup cornmeal

¼ teaspoon kosher salt

½ cup whole milk

⅛ cup heavy cream

1 cup grated farmstead cheddar cheese plus ⅓ cup for topping

2 large eggs, whites and yolks separated

⅛ cup of cream-style corn, canned or homemade

1 tablespoon minced fresh chives

1 small clove garlic, minced

½ teaspoon fresh sage, minced

Green Mountain Gruyere Crisps

4 ounces Green Mountain Gruyere cheese, shredded

Chicken

1 teaspoon kosher salt, or as needed

½ teaspoon white pepper, or as needed

4 (8-ounce) boneless, skin-on chicken breasts, preferably Misty Knoll Farms

1 tablespoon extra-virgin olive oil

¾ cup low sodium chicken stock

2 sprigs fresh thyme

4 ounces Vanilla-Truffle Butter Sauce (see recipe)

2 cups sweet corn spoonbread (see recipe)

Vanilla-Truffle Butter Sauce

1 tablespoon olive oil

⅓ cup minced shallot

½ cup dry white wine

¼ vanilla bean, split in half and seeds scraped, reserve both seeds and pod

1 garlic clove, minced

½ teaspoon white truffle oil

½ cup heavy cream, room temperature

4 ounces unsalted butter, cubed

½ teaspoon kosher salt

¼ teaspoon freshly ground black pepper

Affilla cress or microgreens, trimmed for garnish

continues . . .

1. To prepare the corn: Place a large bowl of water near your cooking area. De-silk the corn ears carefully by pulling the outer husks down to the corn ear's base, removing and discarding the silk, then fold the husks back to their original position around the corn ear to protect it while it grills. Transfer corn to the prepared bowl of water. Repeat with the remaining ear of corn and let soak for 30 minutes.

2. Just before the corn has finished the half-hour soak, heat the grill to medium heat.

3. To make the Gruyere crisps: While the corn is soaking, make the crisps. Preheat the oven to 400°F. Line a half-sheet baking sheet with parchment paper. Place the gruyere cheese in the middle of the prepared baking sheet, then separate it into eight even piles, spacing each about 3 inches apart. Using the flat edge of a knife, lightly pat each pile down to about 3 inches in diameter. The pile should be flat but not pressed.

4. Bake in the oven until bubbly and slightly golden, approximately 5 minutes. During baking, it is important to keep a close eye on the Gruyere crisps to avoid burning. Allow to cool and crisp on the baking sheet until they are needed, remove with an offset spatula. Reduce the oven to 350°F.

5. To roast the corn: Using tongs, remove the corn from the water, shaking off any excess moisture. Place the corn on the grill, cover, and roast, turning once, until corn kernels are fork tender and develops a little char, about 20 minutes. Set corn aside to cool until the chicken has gone into the oven.

6. While the corn is roasting, start the chicken. Season the chicken with salt and white pepper on both sides. Heat the oil in a large ovenproof skillet over medium-high heat until hot but not smoking. Add the chicken breasts, in batches, if necessary, skin side down, and sear, about 4 minutes. Using tongs, turn the pieces over and continue to sear, about 4 minutes. Repeat with the remaining chicken breasts. If working in batches, return all the chicken to the skillet, add the chicken stock and 2 thyme sprigs. Transfer the skillet to the oven and cook until the chicken reaches an internal temperature of 165°F, about 35 to 45 minutes, depending on the size of breasts. Remove from the oven and transfer the chicken to a plate to rest, reserving the stock and thyme in the skillet. The chicken breasts will finish in the oven while the spoonbread bakes and can rest on the counter until the spoonbread is done.

7. To make the spoonbread: When the chicken has gone into the oven and the corn is cool enough to handle, remove the husks and discard. Place the base of an ear of corn in a bowl and using a sharp knife, cut downward, as close to the base of the kernels as possible, into the bowl, turning the ear as you go. Repeat with the remaining corn ear, reserving any juices in the bowl. You should have approximately 1½ cups of roasted corn kernels.

8. Generously grease a 9-inch ovenproof skillet with butter. Set aside. In a small bowl, combine the cornmeal and salt. Set aside.

9. In a 2-quart saucepan, heat the milk and cream to a simmer, stirring occasionally, over medium heat. In a slow and steady stream add the cornmeal, stirring constantly with a wooden spoon until the large clumps are gone. The mixture should be smooth and thick. Remove from the stovetop, then fold in the roasted corn, 1 cup of cheese, 2 egg yolks, cream-style corn, chives, garlic, and sage until well combined.

10. Using a handheld mixer, whip the egg whites until soft peaks form. Stir one-third of the egg whites into the cornmeal mixture, then gently fold in the remaining egg whites until no white streaks remain.

11. Scrape the cornmeal mixture into the prepared skillet, then smooth the top with a spatula. Sprinkle with the remaining ⅓ cup of cheese, then transfer to the oven with the chicken. Bake until puffed and the outer edges have turned a light golden brown, about

25 minutes. The spoonbread has set when the top has become golden and slightly puffed.

12. To make the vanilla truffle butter sauce: The butter sauce should be made as soon as the spoonbread and the chicken are in the oven, as it can tolerate being held at room temperature until the rest of the recipe is done. Heat the oil in a large skillet over medium heat. Add the shallots and cook, stirring often until soft, about 2 minutes. Add the wine, vanilla pod and seeds, garlic, and white truffle oil and bring to a simmer, stirring often, until reduced by half, about 3 minutes. In a slow and steady stream, whisk in the heavy cream and bring to a simmer, stirring often, until reduced by half, about 2 minutes. Reduce the heat to low then stir in the butter, one cube at a time until completely combined.

13. While the butter is melting, reduce the chicken sauce: Transfer the skillet with the reserved stock to the stovetop and reduce the sauce to ¼ cup, whisking often, over medium-high heat, about 4 minutes. Discard the thyme sprigs and adjust the seasonings with salt and pepper.

14. Once all the butter has been incorporated into the vanilla butter sauce, strain through a fine mesh strainer, using a spoon to gently press all the liquids out into a container with a spout. Season with salt and pepper to taste.

15. For assembly: Place a ½ cup of the hot spoonbread in the center of a dinner plate. Rest 1 chicken breast, skin side up on the spoonbread. Using a spoon, drizzle 2 tablespoons of the sauce over and around the chicken, or to taste. Drizzle 2 tablespoons of the vanilla-truffle butter sauce and ½ teaspoon of the honey over and around the chicken, followed by ½ teaspoon of the truffle oil. Place 1 to 2 Gruyere cheese crisp on the side of the chicken breast, then garnish with affilla cress. Repeat with the remaining ingredients.

Note: Affilla Cress is a variety of the sweet pea tendril.

Executive Chef Gregory J. Lang/Preston's Restaurant at Killington Resort

Warm Chicken, Tomato, and Mozzarella Napoleon with Basil Oil and Balsamic Glaze

SERVES 4 TO 6

This recipe makes more basil oil than you will need for the chicken; the remaining oil can be used for salad dressing or a marinade.

1 cup chopped fresh basil

1 cup olive oil

1 cup all-purpose flour

3 large eggs, lightly beaten

2 cups panko bread crumbs

4 skinless, boneless chicken breasts (about 2½ pounds), trimmed and halved lengthwise

3 tablespoons canola or vegetable oil

2 large tomatoes, sliced

1 (8-ounce) ball fresh mozzarella, sliced

Aged balsamic vinegar, for drizzling

1. Preheat the oven to 350°F. Spray a 9-inch square baking dish with nonstick cooking spray and set aside. Combine the basil and olive oil in a small bowl and set aside.

2. Place the flour in a shallow bowl, the eggs in a second bowl, and the panko in a third bowl. Dip each piece of chicken in the flour, then the eggs, and finally the panko. Heat the vegetable oil in a large skillet over medium-high heat until hot but not smoking. Add the chicken in batches and cook until browned, 4 to 5 minutes per side.

3. Arrange half of the chicken in the prepared dish. Layer the tomato slices and cheese slices over the chicken, and then top with the remaining chicken. Bake until the chicken has cooked through and the cheese has melted, about 20 minutes. Drizzle with the basil oil and balsamic vinegar and serve.

West Mountain Inn

Maine Lobster with Celery Root Purée, Blood Oranges, and Hazelnuts

SERVES 4; MAKES 5 CUPS PURÉE

The succulent lobster meat and the subtle bright citrus flavor from the blood oranges provide the perfect counterpoint to the rich, silky consistency of the celery root purée and the nutty notes and crunchy texture from the toasted hazelnuts in this elegant dish.

Lobsters

2 (1¾ pounds each) fresh live Maine lobsters (½ lobster per person)

2 tablespoons unsalted butter, or as needed

Celery Root Purée

2 cups heavy cream

1 cup water

⅛ teaspoon kosher salt plus ½ teaspoon kosher salt, or to taste

2 pounds celery root (about 2 roots), scrubbed, ends removed, peeled, and cut into 1-inch size chunks

1 medium onion, peeled and coarsely chopped into chunks

1 bay leaf

⅛ teaspoon freshly grated nutmeg

Kosher salt and freshly ground black pepper to taste

For Serving

2 ounces whole hazelnuts, toasted and coarsely chopped

½ cup hazelnut butter, or as needed

2 blood oranges, pith and peels removed and cut into supremes (see Tip), reserving any juice

1 teaspoon pink peppercorns, ground into a coarse powder for garnish

2 teaspoons chopped fresh dill for garnish

2 teaspoons chopped fresh cilantro for garnish

Black truffle, shaved, for garnish (optional)

1. To steam the lobsters: Fill a large stockpot with 2 inches of salted water. Bring to a boil. Using tongs, carefully lower the lobsters, one at a time, headfirst into the boiling water. Cover the pot and return the water to a boil, about 4 minutes. Steam until the outer shells of the lobsters turn bright red and an internal temperature of the lobster meat reaches 135°F, about 12 to 18 minutes, depending on the size.

2. While the lobsters are steaming, prepare a work-space to remove the meat from the lobsters by filling a bowl with ice water and placing a rimmed baking sheet nearby. Using tongs, carefully plunge the lobsters into the ice-water bath for about 5 minutes, or until cool enough to handle, replenishing the ice in the bowl of water as necessary. Transfer the chilled lobsters to the rimmed baking sheet.

3. Remove all the meat from the lobsters, keeping claws whole. Chop each tail into four pieces. Pat the lobster meat dry with paper towels, then transfer to a large bowl. Cover with plastic wrap and place in the refrigerator until ready to use.

4. Meanwhile, in a large saucepan, bring the cream, water, and ⅛ teaspoon of salt to just a simmer over medium heat, about 8 minutes. Add the celery root, onion, bay leaf, and nutmeg, and adjust the heat to maintain a simmer, cooking until the vegetables are fork tender, about 20 minutes.

5. While the celery root and onions are simmering, preheat the oven to 375°F.

6. To toast the hazelnuts: Arrange the hazelnuts in a single layer on a baking sheet and toast, stirring occasionally, until the skins are blistered, about 8 minutes. While hot, carefully wrap the nuts in a kitchen towel and vigorously rub to remove the loose skins, then coarsely chop. Not all of the hazelnut skins will come off.

7. To make the celery root purée: Place a large measuring cup in the sink with a pour spout and set a colander over the cup, then drain, reserving the cream mixture and discarding the bay leaf. Place the celery root, onion, ½ teaspoon salt, and ½ teaspoon pepper in a blender, adding the cream mixture as needed, and blend until very smooth, scraping down the sides as needed. Adjust seasonings with salt and pepper to taste. Alternately, return the celery root and onion to the saucepan, adding the cream mixture as needed, and purée with a handheld blender until very smooth. Once the purée has been blended, adjust the seasonings with ½ teaspoon salt and ½ teaspoon pepper, or to taste.

8. To reheat the lobster: In a large saucepan, melt the 2 tablespoons of unsalted butter over low heat. Once the butter has melted, remove the pan from the heat. Add the lobster, basting the pieces with the butter, until fully coated and heated through, about 3 minutes.

9. To assemble: Using a spoon, carefully place some of the celery root purée in the center of four plates. Divide the lobster pieces evenly, placing them around the celery root purée. Place a swoosh of the desired amount of the hazelnut butter on the plates and lightly sprinkle with the pink peppercorns ground into a coarse powder. Scatter the orange segments and crushed hazelnuts around and between the lobster and drizzle with some of the reserved orange juice. Garnish with dill, cilantro, and black truffles, if desired. Serve at once.

Note: Reserve the celery root peel for another use, such as a vegetable stock.

Twin Farms/Executive Chef Nathan Rich

TIP: HOW TO SUPREME AN ORANGE

Start by cutting off the ends of the orange. Using a sharp paring knife, starting at the top, slice as close to the orange flesh as possible to remove the pith and peel by following the curve of the orange in a downward motion. Once the peel and pith are removed, slice off any remaining pith. Hold the orange over a small bowl and cut the orange into supremes, discarding any membranes or seeds, and reserve the orange juice in the bowl.

SMUGGLERS' NOTCH DISTILLERY

Since the first publishing of *The Vermont Farm Table Cookbook*, Smugglers' Notch Distillery, owned and operated in these beautiful green mountains by father-and-son team Ron Elliot (a retired business executive) and Jeremy Elliott (a pharmaceutical chemist), has continued to be an enthusiastic part of Vermont's foodie culture. Four tasting rooms—including one in Burlington, Stowe/Waterbury, Manchester, and at their flagship store at the distillery in Jeffersonville—offer experiences for visitors to learn about the team's story and process.

Smugglers' Notch produces the highest-rated domestic vodka in America. It is made from a combination of sweet corn and winter wheat sourced from Idaho and then blended with Vermont spring water. Because vodka is 60 percent water, this process also sets this product apart from others. Rather than charcoal filtering, the Elliotts use a particulate filter, which allows the vodka to retain some of its natural flavors. Since launching their Double Gold Award-Winning Vodka back in 2010, they have gone on to craft award-winning bourbons, gins, rum, rye, flavored vodka, a Double Gold Award-Winning Vermont Maple Cream Liqueur, and, most recently, Maple Gin. Partnership with a local maple sugaring operation has been key to offering uniquely Vermont flavor profiles, as well as a line of spirit barrel–aged maple syrups.

Grilled Shrimp with Smugglers' Notch Vodka and Mango Cocktail Sauce

SERVES 6

This recipe came to Chef Peter McLyman on a warm summer's day when he wanted to make shrimp cocktail, but did not want to go the traditional route. Taking a cue from the season, he grilled the shrimp and paired it with a cool, refreshing mango sauce, which he spiked with Smugglers' Notch vodka. This sweet and smoky combination has become McLyman's go-to summer shrimp cocktail recipe.

Dried ancho chiles have a wonderful sweet, yet hot flavor, which adds delicious layers to the marinade. You can substitute a dried pasilla chile, if necessary. The versatile cocktail sauce also pairs perfectly with grilled pork tenderloin, grilled chicken breast, or a meaty white fish such as halibut or snapper.

Shrimp and Marinade

2 cups Italian or balsamic vinaigrette

½ cup chopped fresh cilantro leaves

⅓ cup canned diced green chiles, drained

2 tablespoons red pepper flakes

½ dried ancho chile, seeded, deveined, and coarsely chopped

1½ tablespoons hot sauce, such as Sriracha or Tabasco

3 garlic cloves, chopped

2 teaspoons cayenne pepper

2 teaspoons ground cumin

2 teaspoons ground coriander

2 teaspoons chopped fresh ginger

1½ pounds jumbo shrimp (16/20 count), peeled and deveined

Mango Cocktail Sauce

4 medium ripe mangos, peeled, pitted, and sliced

½ cup Smugglers' Notch vodka

2 tablespoons Grand Marnier

1 tablespoon red pepper flakes

1 teaspoon grated fresh ginger

1. To make the shrimp: Process the vinaigrette, cilantro, green chiles, red pepper flakes, ancho, hot sauce, garlic, cayenne, cumin, coriander, and ginger in a blender or food processor until smooth. Transfer the mixture to a large zip-top bag, add the shrimp, seal, and refrigerate for 1 to 3 hours.

2. To make the mango cocktail sauce: While the shrimp is marinating, combine the mangos, vodka, Grand Marnier, red pepper flakes, and ginger in a clean blender or food processor and pulse until almost smooth. Transfer the sauce to a bowl, cover, and refrigerate for at least 1 hour.

3. Preheat a gas or electric grill or heat a grill pan over medium heat. Remove the shrimp from the marinade and grill for about 2 minutes per side.

4. Pour the cocktail sauce into a decorative bowl and place it on a platter. Arrange the shrimp around the bowl and serve.

Chef Peter McLyman for Smugglers' Notch Distillery

WEST MOUNTAIN INN

Nestled on 150 mountainside acres overlooking the Battenkill Valley, the century-old West Mountain Inn has been welcoming travelers with warmth and hospitality for the last 40 years. Dining at the inn is a very important part of a guest's stay. Chef Jeff Scott prepares delicious New England fare with only the freshest ingredients. Everything served by the inn is made on-site using local organic produce, free-range meats and poultry, seasonal game, local cheeses and dairy products, and fresh fish. All the inn's breads, pastries, and desserts are homemade. Working directly with local organic farms and food producers, West Mountain Inn is helping maintain Vermont's rich agricultural heritage and provides a dining experience bursting with freshness and flavor.

Sautéed Sea Scallops in Smoked Bacon and Maple Cream Sauce

SERVES 3 TO 4

Chef Scott uses Vermont Smoke and Cure bacon in this dish. These quick scallops make a perfect hot appetizer, or you can serve them with quinoa and a fresh green vegetable as a main course.

1 tablespoon olive oil

12 large sea scallops, tendons removed

3 ounces (about 3 slices) smoked bacon, minced

½ cup pure Vermont maple syrup

¼ cup heavy cream

Kosher salt and freshly ground black pepper

1. Heat the oil in a large skillet over medium-high heat. Add the scallops and sear for 2 minutes on each side. Transfer to a plate and set aside.

2. Add the bacon to the empty pan and cook for about 1 minute. Add the maple syrup and heat for 1 minute. Slowly whisk in the cream and cook until heated through, about 1 minute. Return the scallops and any accumulated juices to the pan and warm through. Season with salt and pepper to taste and serve.

West Mountain Inn

Pan-Seared Salmon with Crabmeat and Sweet Potato Hash and Tomato Coulis

SERVES 4

The heart of this dish is the crabmeat and sweet potato hash. It was inspired by a cool September day, the colors of fall, and some fresh veggies. Since New England crab is considered some of the best around, Chef Scott wanted to find a way to combine it with local vegetables. The hash and coulis are equally as tasty when paired with any kind of fish.

2 sweet potatoes, peeled and diced

2 tablespoons (1 ounce) unsalted butter

1 medium onion, diced

2 tablespoons chopped garlic

4 medium tomatoes, cored and chopped

1 cup dry white wine

2 tablespoons arrowroot

2 tablespoons cold water

4 (7- to 8-ounce) skinless salmon fillets

1 cup diced red bell pepper

1 cup diced yellow bell pepper

8 ounces fresh crabmeat or frozen and thawed

1 tablespoon chopped fresh thyme

Kosher salt and freshly ground black pepper

1. Place the sweet potatoes in a medium saucepan and cover with cold, salted water. Bring to a boil over high heat and cook until the potatoes are tender, about 10 minutes. Drain and set aside.

2. Melt 1 tablespoon of the butter in a medium skillet over medium heat. Add the onion and stir to coat. Spread the onion in an even layer and cook, stirring occasionally, for 10 minutes. Sprinkle with salt, reduce the heat to medium-low, and continue cooking until the onion is nicely browned, about 10 minutes. Add 1 tablespoon of the garlic and cook for 1 more minute. Add the tomatoes and ½ cup of the wine and cook until the mixture is reduced by one-third, 20 to 25 minutes.

3. Heat the oven to 350°F. In a small bowl, whisk together the arrowroot and water. Whisk into the tomato mixture. Transfer to a food processor and purée until smooth. Season with salt and pepper to taste. Cover and keep warm.

4. Melt the remaining 1 tablespoon of butter in a large skillet over medium-high heat. When the pan is hot, add the salmon and sear about 2 minutes on each side. Transfer the salmon to a baking sheet and bake for 15 minutes.

5. While the salmon is baking, add the peppers and remaining 1 tablespoon garlic to the empty skillet. Cook until the peppers are tender, about 3 minutes. Add the sweet potatoes, crabmeat, thyme, and the remaining ½ cup wine and cook, stirring frequently, until the liquid is reduced by one-third, 10 to 15 minutes. Divide the hash among individual plates, place a salmon fillet on each portion of hash, and top with the tomato coulis. Serve.

West Mountain Inn

WhistlePig Whiskey and Molasses–Marinated Salmon Fillets

SERVES 4

This recipe is a great one to pull out when you are entertaining guests. It is very easy to prepare ahead of time. To prevent the fish from sticking, make sure the grill grate is very clean; scrape or brush it and oil it well just before cooking the salmon.

2 cups molasses

½ cup WhistlePig whiskey

1 tablespoon minced fresh ginger

1 garlic clove, minced

1 cup canola oil, plus extra for the grill

Kosher salt and freshly ground black pepper

4 (7-ounce) skinless salmon fillets

1. In a medium bowl, whisk together the molasses, whiskey, ginger, and garlic. Whisk in the canola oil until well combined. Season with salt and pepper to taste. Place the salmon in a large zip-top bag, pour the marinade over the salmon, seal, and place in the refrigerator for 30 minutes, turning the bag over at least once to marinate evenly.

2. Heat a gas or electric grill to medium-high heat and generously brush the cooking grate with oil. Remove the salmon from the marinade and grill for 3 minutes. Using a large spatula, carefully flip the fillets over and grill for 3 more minutes. Serve.

Chef Peter McLyman for WhistlePig Whiskey

MEAT

EDEN SPECIALTY CIDERS

In April 2007, Eleanor and Albert Leger bought an abandoned dairy farm in West Charleston. A year earlier, while visiting Montreal, they had sampled ice cider and discussed making a similar product in Vermont. The two decided to knock down the decrepit farmhouse and replace it with a new building that would have a full-sized foundation and basement. In the basement of the rebuilt farmhouse, a small pressing operation and bonded winery were born. During the winter of 2007, they made their first batch of about 100 cases of ice cider, which sold out in a month and a half. The demand for their product gave the couple enough confidence to start Eden Orchards and Eden Specialty Ciders.

All of the ciders and ice ciders that Eden produces are made from 100 percent local and sustainably grown apples. The naturally cold weather conditions here concentrate the flavors and sugars of the fruit before fermentation. Envision going to an apple orchard in the fall and sampling a cup of fresh-pressed apple cider. The cider has a rich, sweet yet tart flavor, along with a wonderful apple aroma. This balanced flavor is what Eden's Vermont ice ciders have become known and awarded for. They focus on a product that has a great "apple nose," which gives the palate a wonderful first impression of freshness. The product must also have a balance of acidity for a nice tart finish.

These artisanal producers are dedicated to making a product with thought and care for the climate, community, and the planet on which we live. All their materials are recyclable and renewable.

Pan-Roasted Berkshire Pork Chops with Vermont Ice Cider

SERVES 2

Vermonters are fortunate to have organic pasture-raised Berkshire pork in the area. These pork chops have a wonderful flavor and delicate texture. Apples and pork are natural culinary partners, as the acidity from the apples brightens the subtle meatiness of the pork. Eden Calville Blend Vermont Ice Cider is a perfect pairing for pork, offering a balance of sweetness and acidity. See photo on page 141.

2 (10-ounce) bone-in pork chops,
    1¼ inches thick, trimmed

Sea salt and freshly ground black pepper

Freshly ground black pepper, to taste

1½ tablespoons olive oil

2 tablespoons (1 ounce) unsalted butter

¼ cup minced shallot

1 tablespoon chopped fresh thyme, rosemary, or
    sage, plus 2 sprigs for garnish

⅔ cup Eden Calville Blend Vermont Ice Cider

1. Preheat the oven to 375°F. Season the pork chops with salt and pepper to taste.

2. Heat the oil in a medium ovenproof skillet over medium-high heat until hot, but not smoking. Add the pork chops and brown, about 3 minutes per side. Cover the skillet with aluminum foil, transfer to the oven, and roast until an instant-read thermometer registers 150°F, about 10 minutes.

3. Transfer the pork chops to a plate and tent with foil.

4. Add 1 tablespoon of the butter to the pan juices in the skillet and melt over medium-high heat. Add the shallots and chopped thyme and cook, stirring often, until soft and golden, about 2 minutes. Remove the pan from the heat and carefully add the ice cider. Return the pan to the heat and bring the liquid to a gentle boil. Deglaze the pan, stirring frequently and scraping up bits from the bottom, until the liquid is reduced by half, about 4 minutes. Whisk in the remaining 1 tablespoon of butter until well incorporated. Season with salt and pepper to taste.

5. Place the pork chops on individual plates and spoon some of the sauce over each chop. Garnish with herb sprigs and serve.

Eden Specialty Ciders

WHISTLEPIG WHISKEY

The folks at the WhistlePig Distillery believe that, when it comes to their whiskey, there are many new frontiers to explore. The small craft distillery, located in Shoreham, Vermont, looks to the future with great anticipation and enthusiasm. The farm's dairy barn, situated on the 500-acre property, has been upgraded and converted into a single estate distillery to achieve this goal.

Using grain that is grown on the farm, WhistlePig distills and matures its whiskey in barrels that are made from the property's harvested trees. They are most proud of their Vermont oak barrels. Because of the limitations associated with a small farm distillery, inventory from third party producers is also used. Generally, the distillery produces between 1,500 to 2,000 barrels a year from the grain grown on the farm.

WhistlePig produces one of the leading and most-awarded "farm-to-bottle" rye whiskeys in the world. They have been acknowledged as the #1 distiller in the ultra-premium and luxury rye whiskey category in North America. The folks at WhistlePig are realizing their dream to create amazing whiskey. For them, the awards are secondary to the rewards and quality of their product.

New York Strip Steaks with WhistlePig Whiskey Demi-Glace Sauce

SERVES 4

Chef Peter McLyman received some high-quality New York strip steaks that had some great marbling. He had just tasted WhistlePig Whiskey for the first time earlier that week and thought that it would complement the steaks beautifully. Peter brought some of that straight rye back to the kitchen and created his whiskey demi-glace. You can substitute white mushrooms, portobellos, or stemmed shiitake mushrooms for the cremini.

4 (10-ounce) New York strip steaks, about 1 inch thick, trimmed

Kosher salt and freshly ground black pepper

3 tablespoons olive oil

10 ounces cremini mushrooms, thinly sliced

¼ cup finely chopped shallot

1 garlic clove, minced

⅓ cup WhistlePig whiskey

1¼ cups demi-glace or beef stock

¼ cup heavy cream

1. Preheat the oven to 425°F. Season the steaks generously with salt and pepper.

2. Heat 2 tablespoons of the oil in a large ovenproof skillet over medium-high heat. When the oil is hot, add the steaks and sear 3 to 4 minutes on each side. Transfer the steaks to a baking sheet and bake until medium-rare, 6 minutes.

3. While the steaks are in the oven, add the remaining 1 tablespoon oil to the empty skillet and heat over medium heat. Add the mushrooms, shallot, and garlic and cook for 2 minutes. Remove the skillet from the heat and carefully whisk in the whiskey. Return the skillet to the heat and cook for about 2 minutes. Add the demi-glace and return to a simmer. Slowly whisk in the cream and cook until the sauce is slightly reduced. Season with salt and pepper to taste. Spoon the sauce over the steaks and serve.

Variation: Prepare a gas or electric grill and grill the steaks over medium-high heat, turning once, until medium-rare, 3 to 4 minutes. While the steaks are resting, prepare the whiskey demi-glace sauce in a skillet. Prepare demi-glace just as you would for skillet/oven preparation. Spoon the sauce over the steaks and serve.

Chef Peter McLyman for WhistlePig Whiskey

Panko-Encrusted Minute Steaks

SERVES 4

The gravy in this recipe is very light, almost broth-like, which adds a nice textural contrast to the succulent meat and crispy panko bread crumbs. Add some garlic mashed potatoes and a fresh vegetable, and you've got the perfect country dinner. If possible, buy grass-fed beef for this recipe.

8 (4-ounces each) minute steaks, trimmed

Sea salt and freshly ground black pepper

1 tablespoon unsalted butter

¼ cup plus 1 tablespoon olive oil

3 garlic cloves, minced

1 cup plus 1½ tablespoons all-purpose flour

2 cups low-sodium beef broth

⅛ teaspoon Worcestershire sauce, or to taste

1 tablespoon chopped fresh thyme, or to taste

Pinch cayenne pepper

3 large eggs, lightly beaten

2 cups panko or homemade bread crumbs

1. Place each steak between sheets of parchment paper and, using a meat mallet, pound to ¼-inch thickness. Season the meat with salt and pepper to taste.

2. Heat the butter and 1 tablespoon of the oil in a large skillet over medium heat until hot, but not smoking. Add the garlic and cook for 30 seconds. Add 1½ tablespoons of the flour and cook for 30 seconds. Whisk in the stock, Worcestershire sauce, and thyme, stirring constantly, until smooth and slightly thickened. Pour into a bowl and set aside. Carefully wipe out the pan with a paper towel.

3. In a medium bowl, stir together the remaining 1 cup flour and cayenne pepper. Place the eggs and bread crumbs in separate bowls. Dip each minute steak in the flour, then in the egg, and then in the bread crumbs. Set the steaks on a cooling rack.

4. Heat 2 tablespoons oil in the same skillet used for the sauce over medium-high heat until hot, but not smoking. Add two steaks and cook until the crust is nicely browned on both sides, 2 to 3 minutes per side. Transfer to a platter and repeat with the remaining 2 tablespoons oil and remaining steaks. Let the steaks rest for 5 minutes. While the steaks rest, warm the gravy, then serve the steaks and gravy together.

High Ridge Meadows Farm

SHAT ACRES FARM

The Shatney family has been raising Highland cattle on Shat Acres Farm in Greensboro Bend for over 50 years. They market their beef under the brand name Greenfield Highland Beef. The family has the oldest closed herd in the country, which means that they have not bought a cow in over 40 years, and their herd is the one of the largest herd of Highlands in the United States. Today, the farm is considered to have some of the top Highland cattle genetics in the country.

The success of Shat Acres Farm stems from Carroll Shatney, who had an eye for cattle. He knew which bulls to use and which animals to cull. Carroll loved his Highlands and instilled that love in his son, Ray, who today owns the farm with his wife, Janet Steward.

Being a good steward of the land has always been part of the Shatneys' farm philosophy—"taking care of the land so your animals will have what they need." The owners feel an obligation to make sure that their animals are properly cared for and have a good life. The end result is that consumers have access to humanely raised, high-quality local meat.

Amber Ale–Braised Highland Beef Chuck Roast

SERVES 6

Because there is very little waste with Highland beef, if you are lucky enough to have access to Greenfield Highland Beef, you can use a 2- to 3-pound roast for this recipe; it will still serve six. Pair this roast with mashed potatoes for a delicious meal.

1 (3- to 4-pound) boneless beef chuck roast, trimmed

Kosher salt and freshly ground pepper

¼ cup all-purpose flour

5 tablespoons canola oil

1½ pounds yellow onions, thinly sliced

3 large garlic cloves, minced

1 tablespoon pure Vermont maple syrup

1 tablespoon tomato paste

1½ cups low-sodium beef broth, or as needed

1 (12-ounce) bottle Vermont amber ale

¼ cup apple cider vinegar

2 tablespoons chopped fresh parsley

4 sprigs fresh thyme

1 bay leaf

1½ tablespoons whole-grain Dijon mustard

1½ teaspoons cornstarch

2 tablespoons water

1. Preheat the oven to 325°F. Season the roast with salt and pepper to taste. Place the flour in a large, shallow bowl and dredge the roast in the flour.

2. Heat 3 tablespoons of the oil in a large Dutch oven over medium-high heat until hot but not smoking. Add the meat and brown on all sides, about 5 minutes per side. Transfer to a large plate and set aside.

3. Reduce the heat to medium and add the remaining 2 tablespoons oil. Add the onions and cook until soft and translucent, stirring often, about 8 minutes. Add the garlic, maple syrup, and tomato paste and cook for 1 minute. Add the broth, ale, vinegar, parsley, thyme, and bay leaf, scraping the bottom of the pot to loosen any brown bits.

4. Spread the mustard thinly over the entire roast and return it to the pot along with any accumulated juices. Bring to a boil over medium heat. Cover the pot and transfer it to the oven. Cook until the meat is fork-tender, about 3 hours, turning the roast over halfway through the cooking time.

5. Transfer the roast to a carving board and tent loosely with foil. Discard the bay leaf and thyme sprigs. Using a slotted spoon, transfer the onions to a plate and tent loosely with foil. With a spoon, skim any fat off the surface of the liquid and bring to a boil over medium-high heat. Continue to boil until the sauce is reduced slightly. Combine the cornstarch and water in a small bowl, then whisk the cornstarch slurry into the liquid. Simmer until the liquid thickens, stirring often, about 3 minutes. Season with salt and pepper to taste.

6. Cut the roast into thick slices, against the grain, or pull apart in pieces. Arrange the meat on a platter with the onions and pour a little of the sauce over the top. Serve, passing the remaining sauce at the table.

Tracey Medeiros and Greenfield Highland Beef

THE FROZEN BUTCHER AT SNUG VALLEY FARM

As successful dairy farmers and Holstein breeders, it was a natural transition for the Nottermanns to use their years of experience to raise natural grass-fed, grass-finished steers to sell to consumers. They have been raising grass-fed beef since 1989, which they sell from their farm in Vermont. Pork and lamb are now available as well. Farmers' markets were central to the strengthening of the family's farm.

Fortunately for the Nottermanns, they now have a second generation involved who is transitioning into the ownership of their current operation. Their son Ben was a high school forestry teacher until 2019, when he moved to full-time on the farm. The resulting expansion has been huge and innovative for hundreds of beefers (now black and angus) and an equal number of piggers, all now on sustainably managed land.

In answer to the question "So, how are things now?" the focus is on utilizing the natural grasses to their highest potential. To do this, the farm's beef is moved to fresh grass every day, all grazing season long. This allows the animals to have a positive impact on the grass and soil. Hence, the grass has at least 30 days of rest before it gets grazed again, providing the time for the plant to regrow and restock itself with nutrients.

The farm buys their young beef animals from producers who share the Nottermann's philosophy and commitment to grass-fed beef. The focus is on genetics, which predisposes the beef animal to be successful on a full diet of grass and forage. This method produces the most tender, flavorful, and well-marbled meat possible.

Pigs on pasture serve in the overall goal of sustainable grazing, as well as providing the animals with a happy, healthy life. The porkers rototill land that is then reseeded for new grazing land for the beef, and the piggers have added lots of nutrients in the process. Being fed non-GMO grain, hay, or grass makes for wonderfully tender, juicy pork. During the winter, all of the animals are housed in open, deep-bedded pack barns, the best design for healthy four-footed beings.

The Nottermanns do a sizable wholesale business selling to local co-ops, restaurants, and farmstands all over the northern half of Vermont. When Covid hit, they added online ordering and home deliveries, which are still working well. Helm, Nancy, and Ben did their last farmers' market in 2021, which was a really hard decision. Looking back, Five Corners Market was a foundation builder for them, and they will be forever grateful to Essex Junction, Vermont, for its support. As of 2022, restaurants and other outlets are still going strong; people have developed a taste for healthy meat products.

Rolled Stuffed Beef (Rouladen)

SERVES 4

This recipe is from Swabia, the region in southern Germany where Helm Nottermann grew up. The area consisted of small farms, limited budgets, and great cuisine. Nottermann's mother prepared delicious meals using mostly homegrown ingredients. Helm and his wife, Nancy, enjoy many of his mother's recipes using their own grass-fed beef. They like to use Vermont Smoke and Cure bacon in this recipe. To make slicing the beef easier, place it in the freezer for an hour. Good accompaniments include garlic mashed potatoes, roasted red potatoes, sweet potato fries, or homemade spaetzle.

2 pounds top round or flank steak, trimmed

Kosher salt and freshly ground black pepper

8 ounces bacon, finely chopped

1 large sweet onion, minced

½ cup chopped fresh parsley, plus extra for garnish

⅓ cup Dijon mustard, divided

3 tablespoons canola oil

1¾ cups beef stock

2 tablespoons all-purpose flour

1 cup red wine

1 tablespoon Worcestershire sauce

¼ cup sour cream

1. Cut the steak into two pieces, about 4 by 8 inches each. Then slice each piece in half horizontally, making a total of four thin pieces. Place each piece of meat between sheets of parchment paper and, using a meat mallet, pound to ⅛-inch thickness. Season with salt and pepper to taste.

2. Combine the bacon, onion, and parsley in a small bowl. Spread each piece of meat with 4 teaspoons of mustard, then divide the bacon mixture among the four pieces and spread out to cover the mustard. Loosely roll up the beef pieces lengthwise, being careful to keep the mixture inside of the bundles. Carefully tie each roll with butcher's twine, securing the ends and center portion to form an even oblong shape, or secure with toothpicks.

3. Heat the oil in a large Dutch oven over medium-high heat. Add two of the beef rolls and brown on all sides, about 2 minutes per side. Transfer to a platter and repeat with the remaining two rolls. Reduce the heat to medium and add ¼ cup stock to the pot. Scrape up any browned bits and and whisk in the flour until it has absorbed all of the drippings. Whisk in the wine, Worcestershire sauce, and remaining stock until smooth. Return the beef rolls along with any accumulated juices to the Dutch oven, cover, and reduce the heat to low. Simmer for 1½ hours.

4. Transfer the beef rolls to a warm platter. Whisk the sour cream into the broth mixture until smooth. Pour the sauce over the beef, sprinkle with parsley, and serve.

Helm Nottermann of Snug Valley Farm

VERMONT SALUMI

Peter Roscini Colman's experience in life, and passion for food, was the inspiration for his business, Vermont Salumi. Born in Assisi, in the Umbrian region of Italy, Peter moved to Vermont when he was 3½ years old, where he was raised on an organic vegetable farm. Growing up, Peter split his time between working on his family's Cate Farm in Plainfield and taking annual trips to Italy to visit other family members. Peter always loved eating prosciutto while in Italy, but he felt it was an expensive product. It was during one of those visits to Italy that Peter decided to learn how to cure his own meat. He expressed this desire to some of his family and friends, who recommended that Peter apply for apprenticeships with old-world butchers in Italy. Peter soon found himself in a butcher shop in Italy, learning how to slaughter pigs and cure the meat.

Upon his return to Vermont, Peter felt that the state offered a business opportunity for dry-curing meats. Using the advanced curing techniques that he learned in Italy, Peter renovated the space in his family's barn to start Vermont Salumi. The company currently offers six types of sausages, which are made from local pork that is raised on pasture without hormones or antibiotics. The sausages are made by hand, in small batches, without the use of nitrates or preservatives.

VERMONT SALUMI

Lentils with Vermont Salumi Daily Grind Sausages

SERVES 4

If you cannot find Vermont Salumi Daily Grind sausages, sweet Italian sausage is a fine substitute. Serve with a loaf of crusty bread.

1 pound Vermont Salumi Daily Grind sausages

6 cups water

1 tablespoon unsalted butter

1 small onion, minced

12 ounces French green lentils

1 bay leaf

Kosher salt and freshly ground black pepper

2 tablespoons olive oil, plus extra for drizzling

2 garlic cloves, minced

1 cup crushed tomatoes

1 tablespoon red wine vinegar

Chopped fresh parsley

1. Bring the sausages and 2 cups of the water to a simmer over medium heat. Cook, turning occasionally, until the sausages are plump and the water has reduced by half, about 12 minutes. Remove the sausages from the stovetop and tent with foil. Reserve 1 cup of the sausage liquid.

2. Melt the butter in a 2½-quart saucepan over medium heat. Add the onion and sauté until soft and translucent, stirring often, about 10 minutes. Add the lentils, the remaining 4 cups water, the bay leaf, and just enough reserved sausage liquid to cover. Increase the heat to medium-high and bring to a boil. Reduce the heat to medium-low, partially cover, and simmer until tender, about 1 hour. Discard the bay leaf. Season with salt and pepper to taste. Cover and set aside.

3. Heat the oil in a medium skillet over medium heat. Add the sausages and cook until browned, about 6 minutes. Add the garlic and cook for 1 minute, stirring often. Transfer the garlic, tomatoes, and vinegar to the lentil pot and cook until heated through. Season with salt and pepper to taste.

4. Slice the sausages and arrange them over the warm lentils. Drizzle olive oil over the top and sprinkle with parsley. Serve.

Vermont Salumi

Berkshire Pork Loin with Poached Apples

SERVES 6

The key to this roast's juiciness is that it brines overnight, so be sure to start this recipe the day before you plan to serve it. Pork tenderloins can be used in place of the roast; just reduce the brining time to six hours. The poached apples can be made a day in advance. Refrigerate the apples and poaching liquid separately, then recombine and reheat them before serving.

Pork

½ cup apple brandy

½ cup whole-grain mustard

½ cup wildflower honey

¼ cup salt

1 tablespoon chopped fresh sage

4 cups water

3 pounds boneless pork loin, trimmed

2 tablespoons olive oil

Poached Apples

8 cups Vermont apple cider

½ cup granulated sugar

½ cup dry white wine

1 small sprig fresh rosemary

½ vanilla bean, split

6 apples such as Cortland, Empire, or Granny Smith, peeled

Chopped fresh rosemary

Apple-Thyme Sauce (optional; recipe follows)

1. To make the pork: Whisk together the brandy, mustard, honey, salt, and sage in a large container until smooth. Whisk in the water. Submerge the loin, cover the container, and refrigerate overnight.

2. To make the poached apples: Combine the cider, sugar, wine, rosemary, and vanilla bean in a large stockpot. Add the apples, cover and bring to a boil over medium heat. Remove the rosemary and let cool for 1 hour. When the apples are cool, core and slice them and set aside. Reserve ½ cup plus 2 table-spoons of the poaching liquid if making the sauce.

3. Preheat the oven to 425°F. Set a rack in a roast-ing pan. Remove the pork from the brine and pat dry with a towel. Brush pork with oil and place on the roasting rack.

4. Roast the pork until it begins to brown, about 15 minutes. Lower the heat to 350°F and cook until the internal temperature reaches 135°F. Let rest for 15 minutes, then slice. Garnish the pork with the sliced apples, sprinkle with chopped rosemary, drizzle with the Apple-Thyme Sauce, if desired, and serve.

APPLE-THYME SAUCE

2½ cups veal stock or chicken stock

½ cup plus 2 tablespoons apple poaching liquid

1 sprig fresh thyme

2 teaspoons arrowroot

2 tablespoons (1 ounce) unsalted butter

Kosher salt

Combine veal stock, ½ cup of the poaching liquid, and thyme sprig in a medium saucepan and bring to a simmer over medium-low heat. In a small bowl, combine the arrowroot and the last 2 tablespoons poaching liquid. Whisk arrowroot mixture into stock and cook until slightly thickened, about 15 minutes. Whisk in butter. Discard thyme sprig and season with salt to taste.

Odyssey Events

JERICHO SETTLERS FARM

Christa Alexander and Mark Fasching started their year-round, diversified farm on leased land back in 2002. Today, they are proud owners of this land and Jericho Settlers Farm has grown to encompass 150 sprawling acres in the towns of Jericho and Richmond.

Alexander and Fasching offer a year-round CSA and farm stand and work with a small number of local chefs and restaurants. They embrace the daily, and seasonal, challenges that come with farming.

Cider-Braised Pork Chops with Apples and Onions

SERVES 6

It is very important to purchase bone-in blade-cut pork chops and not bone-in center-cut chops for this dish. The blade-cut pork chops will be tender and falling off the bone, rather than overcooked and tough. Serve with a fresh green vegetable such as kale or broccoli rabe and crusty bread on the side.

6 bone-in blade-cut pork chops, 1 inch thick, trimmed

Kosher salt and freshly ground black pepper

2 tablespoons olive oil

2 medium yellow onions, chopped

2 apples, such as Empire, Cortland, or McIntosh, cored and coarsely chopped

1 cup Vermont apple cider

½ cup chicken stock

2 tablespoons pure Vermont maple syrup

3 garlic cloves, minced

2 sprigs fresh thyme, plus extra sprigs for garnish

1. Preheat the oven to 300°F. Season the pork chops with salt and pepper to taste. Heat the oil in a large Dutch oven over medium-high heat. Add the chops and brown on both sides, in batches, about 2 minutes per side. Transfer the pork chops to a plate and set aside.

2. Reduce the heat to medium. Add the onions to the pot and cook, stirring often, until soft and golden, about 6 minutes. Add the apples, cider, stock, maple syrup, garlic, and thyme, stirring until well combined. Bring to a boil and continue to cook, whisking often, until the sauce is slightly reduced. Return the pork chops and accumulated juices to the pot. Cover and cook until the meat is tender and falling off the bone, about 1 hour. Season with salt and pepper to taste.

3. Place the pork chops on individual plates and arrange the apples and onions around the meat. Top with the sauce and garnish with thyme sprigs. Serve.

Jericho Settlers Farm

MISERY LOVES CO.

Misery Loves Co. is a brick-and-mortar establishment located in downtown Winooski, Vermont. It operates as a market and restaurant with a menu that offers a variety of choices for lunch and dinner. Laura Wade and Aaron Josinsky are the co-owners. Aaron is the restaurant's chef, creating innovative spins on American comfort food and craft cocktails.

The market area of the business is filled with food, drinks, and housewares. Visitors can buy fresh bread, house-made foods, pantry provisions, fine chocolate, little house plants, and an assortment of other curiosities. When the weather cooperates, folks can sit outside and relax on the patio while enjoying a delicious cocktail, beer, wine, or glass of cider.

Korean Reuben

SERVES 8 TO 10

This recipe requires a smoker and some advance planning; the brisket must be started five days before it's served. The results are well worth the time and effort, however, for a quick version of this recipe, you can use a good-quality black pastrami.

Brine and Brisket

8½ cups water

1½ cups kosher salt

1 cup granulated sugar

3 tablespoons Insta Cure no. 1 (for slow-cooking meats)

1 garlic head

1 tablespoon pickling spice

2½ pounds fatty point brisket, trimmed

2 teaspoons freshly ground black pepper

2 teaspoons ground coriander

Pickled Mustard Seeds

¾ cup water

¾ cup rice wine vinegar

½ cup mustard seeds

¼ cup granulated sugar

1½ teaspoons kosher salt

Chili Mayo

1 cup mayonnaise, preferably Kewpie (Japanese mayonnaise)

2 tablespoons gochujang, or to taste

16–20 slices hearty rye bread

1 (15-ounce) jar kimchi

1. To brine the brisket: Combine the water, salt, sugar, Insta Cure, garlic, and pickling spice in a large stockpot and bring to a boil over medium-high heat. Let cool, then refrigerate until the brine is cold. Place the brisket in the brine, cover, and refrigerate for 3 days, turning the meat halfway through brining. Remove the meat from the brine and refrigerate, uncovered, overnight.

2. Set up the smoker according to the manufacturer's directions, using apple wood. Coat the meat with the pepper and coriander, place it in the smoker, and smoke slowly, maintaining a temperature of about 200°F, until the internal temperature of the meat reaches 150°F, about 8 hours.

3. When the meat is almost at 150°F, preheat the oven to 325°F. Transfer the meat to the oven and cook until the internal temperature of the meat reaches 190°F, about 45 minutes. Let the brisket cool, then wrap and refrigerate overnight.

4. To make the pickled mustard seeds: Combine the water, vinegar, mustard seeds, sugar, and salt in a medium saucepan and bring to a simmer over medium-low heat, stirring often, until the seeds are plump and tender and the liquid is absorbed, 25 to 30 minutes.

5. To make the chili mayo: Combine the mayonnaise, ¼ cup of the pickled mustard seeds, and gochujang in a small bowl. Add additional mustard seeds to taste.

6. Slice the brisket against the grain. Spread each slice of bread with chili mayo. Layer the brisket and kimchi on half of the bread slices and top with the remaining bread slices. Serve.

Note: Insta Cure No. 1, a blend of salt and sodium nitrite, is available at sausagemaker.com or on Amazon. Gochujang is a chile-spice paste from Korea. It is sold at Asian markets, and some natural food stores. Chili garlic sauce, while not the same, can be substituted.

Misery Loves Co.

BOYDEN VALLEY WINERY & SPIRITS

Boyden Valley Winery & Spirits, housed in a restored 1875 carriage barn on the Boyden family farm in Cambridge, is steeped in the culture and agricultural heritage of Vermont's Green Mountains. From the grapevines that have been lovingly tended by the family for four generations, the Boydens craft wines that feature only the finest fruit from the loamy soils of the Lamoille River Valley. The care with which they've nurtured the land lends itself to traditional winemaking, and the wines they produce are balanced and delicious.

The winery crafts a variety of high-quality international award-winning wines as well as ice wines and cream liqueurs. They welcome visitors year-round to taste their products and learn why they are making Vermont famous for wine.

Pork Tenderloin with Cassis and Soy Sauce Reduction

SERVES 4

The pork tenderloin with cassis and soy sauce reduction recipe was inspired by the winery's cassis wine. Made with Vermont-grown organic grown black currants, the cassis is aged in French oak barrels for two years, making it decadent and pleasing to the palate. Linda Boyden, who is originally from Montreal, created this dish as a reflection of her heritage, combining the rich and savory flavors found in traditional French fare. The sautéed fennel adds a great dimension with a nice sweetness and texture. The cassis (the French term for black currant wine) is aromatic and very flavorful—its fruitiness emerges nicely and lends an elegant soft finish to the sauce.

2 tablespoons olive oil

1 medium fennel bulb, top removed, cored, and thinly sliced, plus 2 tablespoons chopped fronds for garnish

½ teaspoon red pepper flakes

1 pork tenderloin (about 1¼ pounds), trimmed

½ cup low-sodium soy sauce

1 cup pure Vermont maple syrup

½ cup black currant wine,

1 tablespoon unsalted butter

Kosher salt and freshly ground black pepper

1. Heat 1 tablespoon of the oil in a medium skillet over medium heat. Add the fennel and red pepper flakes and toss to coat with the oil. Cook the fennel, stirring occasionally, until soft, about 30 minutes. Season with salt and pepper to taste. Remove from the heat, cover, and set aside.

2. Heat the remaining 1 tablespoon oil in a separate medium skillet over high heat. Season the pork with salt and pepper to taste, place in the skillet, and brown on all sides, about 3 minutes per side. Reduce the heat to medium-low, cover, and cook until an instant-read thermometer registers 145°F, about 20 minutes. Transfer the pork to a plate and tent with aluminum foil.

3. Pour the soy sauce and maple syrup into the same skillet used for the pork. Cook, whisking frequently, over medium-low heat until the liquid is reduced by half, about 5 minutes. Increase the heat to medium-high and slowly whisk in the wine. When the sauce begins to boil, reduce the heat to medium and slowly whisk in the butter. Cook until the mixture is thick enough to coat the back of a spoon, 2 to 3 minutes. Add the fennel and cook just until heated through. Season with salt and pepper to taste.

4. Transfer the pork to a cutting board and cut into ½-inch-thick diagonal slices. Pour the sauce over pork, sprinkle with the reserved fennel fronds, and serve.

Boyden Valley Winery & Spirits

ROMA'S BUTCHERY

There were many work-related experiences along the road of life before Elizabeth Roma, owner of Roma's Butchery, realized her professional dream. After graduating from Green Mountain College in 2007, she decided to farm pigs to learn more about meat processing techniques. This path led to a job at a butcher shop where she worked at the packing and labeling table, familiarizing herself with that end of the business. During this period, she took a month off to travel to Italy to observe the Italian way of meat processing, while also acquiring skills in the art of charcuterie.

In 2014, Roma and her husband bought a 140-acre farm in South Royalton, Vermont, which they named "Putting Down Roots." It was the perfect home for the couple of livestock farmers. At that point, Elizabeth Roma had gained experience with breaking down whole animals into retail cuts, as well as smoking and sausage techniques, at a butcher shop in Maine. Her background now covered working in every step of meat production—farming to slaughter, meat cutting, and smoking. In October 2020, she opened a meat-cutting facility in Royalton, Vermont, soon followed by the addition of a retail butcher shop in March 2021.

The meat that is sold in the butcher shop is processed in what is known as "The Break Room," a custom meat-cutting facility located under the retail shop. Both facilities are state inspected. Roma's business is one of a group of licensed custom meat processors who sell professionally cut meat that is raised locally. The demand for this type of product is rapidly increasing.

Because Roma buys directly from local farms, she finds it extremely important to get to know the farmers that she deals with and the animals that they raise. After she purchases their product, an arrangement is made for slaughter, thereby guaranteeing that the meats are the freshest they can be. The butcher could procure her meat from other locations, but because of their superior quality, has chosen Vermont raised animals. This hands-on approach has enabled Roma to develop strong connections with the farmers that she works with. By supporting local farms and area enterprises, Elizabeth Roma is showing folks what Vermont is all about.

La Picante Sausage

MAKES 5 POUNDS OF SAUSAGE,
ABOUT 16 TO 20 LINKS, DEPENDING ON
THE SIZE OF THE LINKS

The boneless Boston butt is the best cut for this sausage recipe because it has a nice lean-to-fat ratio. We use a course grinder plate to grind the meat. If you don't own a sausage pricker, you could use a sharp toothpick, sewing needle, or the pointy end of a wine corkscrew.

10 feet medium hog casing, or as
    needed for stuffing (see Note)

5 pounds boneless Boston butt

Olive oil for greasing baking sheet, sausage-
    stuffing attachment, and hands

1 cup fresh chopped cilantro,
    small stems and leaves

Zest from 1 lime

¼ cup fresh lime juice

1½ tablespoons kosher salt

1 teaspoon cumin

1 teaspoon coriander

½ tablespoon chili

1½ teaspoons cayenne

¾ tablespoon red pepper flakes

1 tablespoon Aleppo

⅓ cup finely chopped fresh jalapeños, stemmed
    and seeded (about 7 average-sized jalapeños)

1. Preparing the casings: Soak and flush the casings according to your butcher's directions.

2. Preparing the meat for grinding: Line a baking sheet with parchment paper and set aside. Cut the meat and any fat into 1-inch cubes and place on the prepared baking sheet. Transfer to the freezer for 30 minutes. Place the coarse grinder plate and a bowl for catching the ground meat in the refrigerator until cold to the touch.

3. Just before you are ready to grind the meat, place a large bowl of ice near your workstation.

4. To grind the meat: Set the chilled bowl for catching the ground meat on top of the prepared bowl of ice. Replace the cold grinder parts onto the grinder. Push the chilled meat through the grinder one piece at a time until all the meat has been ground.

5. Using food safety gloves, add all the seasonings to the meat and knead with your hands until well combined, then prepare the meat for a second grinding.

6. To prepare the meat for a second grinding: Spread the pork out evenly on the same baking sheet and parchment paper that the meat was on before. Place the ground pork into the freezer for 30 minutes. Place the medium grinder plate and a clean bowl in the refrigerator until cold to the touch, about 30 minutes.

7. Just before the second grinding, change the grinder plate to medium. Place a large fresh bowl of ice near your workstation. Grind the pork a second time then transfer to the freezer once more for 30 minutes.

8. To stuff and link the sausage: Oil the sausage-stuffing attachment, your hands and the same baking sheet that the meat was on before with olive oil. Stuff the sausage according to the manufacturer's instructions, making sure to prick any air bubbles with a sausage pricker, and twist off into approximately 3- to 4-inch lengths. See How to Stuff and Link Your Sausage found on page 164.

9. Place one cooling rack over one rimmed baking sheet and set aside.

10. Once all the sausages have been made, arrange the links in a single layer on the prepared cooling rack and refrigerate overnight, uncovered, turning the sausages occasionally.

11. Using sharp kitchen shears, cut the links and use within 2 days or wrap links individually and place in freezer bags and store in the freezer for up to 2 months.

12. Cook the sausages as desired to an internal temperature of 160°F.

Roma's Butchery

TIPS: WHERE TO BUY CASINGS AND HOW TO PREP

As a rule of thumb, purchase 2 feet of casing per 1 pound of meat. Ask your butcher if they are willing to sell you some casings. It is important to ask the butcher if the casings have been already soaked and prepped. If soaked and prepped, you will need to use them within a day. It should be noted that some of the casings available on the market may need up to 12 hours to soak and rinse.

NOTES: The shorter the sausages, the tighter the pressure of the meat and air inside the casings, and if the pressure is too great (any smaller than 3 inches) there is a risk to rupturing the casing.

If you want less of a spicy kick, feel free to omit the red pepper flakes.

HOW TO STUFF AND LINK YOUR SAUSAGE
Sarah Strauss

It is recommended to read through these steps entirely before making the La Picante Sausage recipe (page 162) so the stuffing process can move very quickly.

1. Chill the sausage-stuffing attachment in the refrigerator before starting the stuffing process.

2. Set up a baking sheet that has been oiled with extra-virgin olive oil so that the sausage can be laid and coiled on the baking sheet as it is stuffed. Oil the outside surface of the chilled stuffer attachment with extra-virgin olive oil so that the casing will slip on easily. Using the oiled baking sheet as a work surface, find an end to the casing, and gently open the end of the casing membrane up into a tube without tearing the membrane.

3. Insert the sausage-stuffing attachment into the casing so that the membrane tube can slide around the tip of the attachment. Very gently, without tearing the casing, thread the stuffer attachment all the way through the casing, carefully scrunching the casing to the bottom of the stuffer attachment as it is loaded on. Use the last 3 to 4 inches of the casing to tie a knot, so that the sausage will stay in the casing and not escape as it is stuffed. Once the casing is scrunched onto the stuffer attachment, attach the sausage-stuffing attachment to your grinder.

4. Oil your hands lightly with extra-virgin olive oil so that they are slippery. Working slowly, stuff the sausage into the casing, focusing on feeding the stuffer at an even speed so that the sausage will be evenly filled. Keep one hand for working the grinder and helping the casing to slip off of the sausage-stuffing attachment at a consistent speed. With your other hand, guide the filled sausage to the oiled baking sheet. If the sausage is stuffed too loosely, there will be too many air bubbles, and if the sausage is stuffed too tightly, it will crack open when cooked.

5. When the ground meat is all gone, and the sausage has been stuffed, pinch the meat through the walls of the casing so that there is about 3 to 4 inches of empty casing. Cut the casing here and tie a small knot to finish the long sausage.

6. At this point, begin to twist the sausage into the desired sizes. Start in the middle of the long snake of sausage, as starting in the middle will help to evenly distribute the meat and any air causing pressure inside the casing. Pinch the meat through the walls of the casing, and then gently twist the sausage to create a segment. Be sure to twist each sausage segment at least four times, so that the segments have enough space between them, and the casing will not untwist when they are cut apart later on. Working from the middle to the ends, pinch and then twist. Sausage segments can be any length desired but should be no shorter than 3 inches long.

7. Once the sausage is segmented, take a sausage pricker (or a sharp toothpick or a sewing needle or the pointy end of a wine corkscrew) and gently pierce any air bubbles that are visible.

MOON AND STARS AREPAS

Moon and Stars is an organization based in Vermont's Upper Valley whose mission is to connect communities, traditional food, and regenerative farming through heirloom corn and the arepa making process. They strive to provide nutrient dense and culturally vital food by creating new ideas about cultural and environmental sustainability.

An arepa is a round patty made of ground corn. They are a staple in Columbia and Venezuela. Traditional arepas are made with heirloom native open pollinated corn, specific to each region of the Andes. Characteristics vary by color, flavor, size, and thickness depending on the region. An arepa can be topped or filled with vegetables, eggs, cheese, hogao (tomatoes and scallions sauteed in olive oil), and beans. The goal of Moon and Stars is to partner with like-minded small farms and markets to source ethically grown produce, which can be used to create their recipes. By doing so, it decreases the dependence on industrial agriculture and reduces our carbon footprint.

The sale of arepas from the Moon and Stars' food cart offers a platform for education. The organization wants people to eat fresh, nutritious food while learning where their food comes from. The goal is to share the corn's story while also introducing Columbian foods such as arepas, empanadas, salsa, and more. With the sale of their arepas, Moon and Stars aims to provide a platform for practices and products that will support local farmers and enhance local and regional markets.

Arepas with Columbian-Style Powdered Beef (Carne en Polvo), Columbian Creole Sauce (Hogao Casero), and White Rice

SERVES 8; MAKES 2 CUPS OF SAUCE AND 6 CUPS OF RICE

Arepas are round savory corn cakes that can be found in Latin American food shops and some grocery stores. This South American staple is very popular in Columbia and Venezuela. Columbian-style powdered beef is a classic dish in Columbia and pairs well with the arepas.

Columbian-Style Powdered Beef

3 pounds top round or flank steak,
  cut into ¼-pound chunks

1¾ teaspoon kosher salt, divided or as needed

1 teaspoon freshly ground black
  pepper, divided or as needed

1 large tomato, cut into large chunks

1 poblano pepper, stemmed and
  seeded, cut into large chunks

2 large cloves garlic, crushed

6 cups water, or as needed to cover the
  meat completely in the pot

2 teaspoons ground cumin, or to taste

½ cup finely crumbled queso fresco or cotija

Columbian Creole Sauce

3 tablespoons olive oil

1 cup (8 medium to large) finely chopped
  scallions, white and green parts

2 cups diced tomatoes, fresh heirloom or
  canned (reserving juices for recipe)

½ teaspoon kosher salt, or as needed

White Rice

2 cups long grain white rice, rinsed

4 cups reserved broth

Kosher salt as needed

8 arepas

1 lime, cut into 8 wedges for serving

½ cup fresh minced cilantro

1. To make the Columbian-style powdered beef: Season the meat with ¾ teaspoon salt and ½ teaspoon pepper.

2. Place the meat, tomato, poblano pepper, garlic, and water in a large pot or Dutch oven. Make sure to add enough water to cover the meat completely in the pot. Cover and bring to a boil over medium-high heat, then reduce the heat to medium-low and continue to cook until the meat is cooked through, about 50 minutes.

3. Using tongs or a slotted spoon, carefully remove the meat from the pot and set aside to cool completely. Strain the broth through a fine-mesh strainer into a clean, heat-resistant bowl, discarding the vegetable solids. Adjust seasonings with salt and pepper, then cover and refrigerate overnight.

4. Once cooled, transfer the meat to a container with a lid and place in the refrigerator overnight.

5. Forty minutes before you plan to serve the beef, make the Columbian Creole Sauce. Heat the oil in a 10-inch skillet over medium heat. Add the scallions and tomatoes and sauté for about 5 minutes. Reduce the heat to a simmer and cook, stirring occasionally, until the sauce has thickened a bit, about 45 minutes, depending on the juice content of the tomatoes. Adjust seasonings with salt to taste. Set aside until ready to use.

6. While the Columbian Creole Sauce is thickening, prepare the beef. Pat the meat dry with paper towels. Place the beef chunks in a food processor and process until the beef has a powdery texture, about 9 minutes. Transfer the beef, cumin, the remaining 1 teaspoon salt, and the remaining ½ teaspoon pepper to a 12-inch nonstick skillet and cook over low heat. Set aside approximately 1 cup of the Colombian Creole Sauce for serving at the table. Add the remaining Columbian Creole Sauce to the beef, 1 tablespoon at a time, while maintaining the dry texture of the beef and continue to cook, stirring frequently, for about 25 minutes. It is important for each tablespoon of sauce to be absorbed before the next one is added. Adjust seasonings with cumin, salt, and pepper to taste. The beef absorbs the moisture from the sauce quickly. It is important to constantly stir and allow each tablespoon of sauce to be fully absorbed before adding the next tablespoon. It is fine if the beef becomes slightly darker as it dries out.

7. While the beef is cooking in the skillet, prepare the rice according to the package instructions, substituting the suggested water for the reserved broth. Defat the broth before using in the rice.

8. To prepare the arepas: Heat the arepas according to the package instructions. While the rice is resting, cut the arepas in half and stuff with some of the meat and top with the reserved Columbian Creole Sauce and queso fresco cheese to taste; serve with rice on the side and lime wedges. Garnish with cilantro.

Note: If using Moon and Stars arepas, lightly butter the tops of the arepas and top with the desired amount of meat, Columbian Creole Sauce, and queso fresco to taste. Serve with rice on the side and lime wedges. Garnish with cilantro. For those who enjoy a lot of Columbian Creole Sauce, feel free to double the recipe.

Moon and Stars Arepas

CONDIMENTS, SALSAS, AND SAUCES

BLACKBERRY-BLUEBERRY JAM

Organic Ingredients:
blackberries; blueberries,
sugar, lemon;
with fruit pectin
CERTIFIED BY VOF
-1224538(-
www.SunshineValleyBerryFarm.com

Blackberry-Blueberry Jam

MAKES 10 HALF-PINT JARS

Pomona's Universal Pectin (an all-natural pectin) is available in most natural foods stores. Each box of pectin contains a packet of calcium powder and directions for making calcium water, which you will need for this recipe. If possible, use organic blueberries, blackberries, and lemons for this jam. Unopened, the jam will last up to nine months. After opening, it should be refrigerated and used within three weeks.

1¾ cups organic cane sugar

4 teaspoons Pomona's Universal Pectin

4 pints blueberries

2 pints blackberries

½ cup fresh lemon juice (3 lemons)

4 teaspoons calcium water

1. Wash ten ½-pint glass jam jars and lids. Place the jars in two large pots, such as stockpots or canning pots, and cover with water. Bring to a boil, then reduce the heat to the lowest setting, letting the jars and lids remain in hot water until ready to use.

2. In a small bowl, stir together the sugar and pectin. Place the blueberries and blackberries in a blender and crush.

3. Transfer the berries to a large saucepan, add the lemon juice and calcium water, and bring to a boil over medium-high heat, stirring constantly. Stir in the sugar-pectin mixture and return to a boil for about 2 minutes, stirring constantly. Remove from the heat and skim off any foam.

4. Remove the jars from the hot water and let air-dry. Carefully ladle the hot jam into the hot glass jars, leaving ¼-inch space at top. Remove any air bubbles and place the hot (dried) lids on the jars and twist as tightly as possible when closing.

5. Arrange the jars in a single layer in the two pots, cover them with hot water, and bring to a boil. Boil for 12 minutes, then immediately remove the jars and set them on a cooling rack or towel. (As the jars cool, the lids will become visibly concave; often there is an audible pop when they seal.) Let sit for at least 12 hours before moving or serving so that the jam will have time to set.

Sunshine Valley Berry Farm

THE VERMONT CRANBERRY COMPANY

The Vermont Cranberry Company, located in Fletcher, is the first commercial grower of cranberries in Vermont. Bob Lesnikoski, essentially a self-taught grower, found his niche growing cranberries back in 1966. Bob was a logging contractor who was looking for another profession, specifically something hands-on involving food. At that time, the cranberry industry was expanding from Massachusetts to Maine. During his job transition, Bob decided to meet some of the growers in Maine to see if the berries would be a good fit for his property. After speaking with them, he decided to give the fruit a try. It wasn't long before he was selling his berries to local restaurants and at nearby farmers' markets.

Today, his company continues to be successful with help from his wife, Elizabeth, and their three children who assist with growing, harvesting, and meticulously hand-sorting their premium berries for color and size. The whole family packs the fruit almost every day. Then Bob, better known to Vermont locals as "Cranberry Bob," delivers them throughout Vermont. They are pretty tired by the time the holiday season rolls around. However, it is rewarding for the Lesnikoski family to sit down at the table during their Thanksgiving meal and think about all the people throughout Vermont who are enjoying their cranberries.

On a little less than 3 acres, the company produces just over 20,000 pounds of cranberries annually from its three producing man-made bogs. The bulk of their sales are fresh fruit for the holiday season. They are small growers, so Bob can grow fruit using the cultural practices that were developed before chemical inputs became common—one example being hand weeding. The company's mission is to produce sustainably grown cranberries in Vermont.

One of the reasons Bob changed from the forest product industry to farming (particularly with a perennial fruit crop such as cranberries) is because it enables him to be personally invested in his property, cranberry beds, and fields. Bob shares, "If done right, these plants are going to outlive me and hopefully, a family member, or another young farmer, will continue my efforts. These cranberries will be my legacy, which is very important to me."

Vermont Cranberry Sauce

SERVES 4

If stored in the refrigerator, this sauce can be made up to one week prior to serving. Use more or less sugar depending on your tastes. For a slight twist, you can substitute Vermont maple syrup or honey for the sugar—the only difference is that the sauce may not gel as well.

¾ cup Vermont apple cider

¾ to 1 cup granulated or packed brown sugar

⅛ teaspoon salt

12 ounces fresh Vermont cranberries

Combine the cider, sugar, and salt in a medium saucepan and bring to a boil over medium-high heat, stirring often. Reduce the heat to a simmer and stir in the cranberries. Cook, uncovered, until the cranberries have popped and the liquid has slightly reduced, stirring occasionally, about 5 minutes. Let cool to room temperature. Transfer to a serving dish and serve, or refrigerate until needed.

Vermont Cranberry Company

CAFÉ MAMAJUANA

During her childhood, Maria Lara-Bregatta, spent many hours at her parents' Tapas Restaurant in South Jersey. It was during those early years that she learned a bit about the workings of a restaurant's kitchen, a good foundation for future culinary endeavors. After perfecting her skills as a chef, she opted to start her own restaurant in Burlington, Vermont. The eatery, Café Mamajuana, opened its doors in November 2020. Coming from a mixed family of Italians and Dominicans, Lara-Bregatta considers the name, Café Mamajuana, to be the perfect fit for the establishment. Mamajuana is the national drink of the Dominican Republic. Prepared in a glass bottle, rum, red wine, and honey are infused with tree bark, herbs, and spices to create this popular beverage.

Lara-Bregatta hopes to connect folks with Dominican, Afro-Caribbean, Italian, and Spanish cultures through the ethnic foods that she serves at her café. The menu is extensive and varies weekly, with offerings such as empanadas, arepas, paella, sweet plantains, and bowls of fresh tropical fruit topped off by a mouthwatering selection of house-made desserts. In consideration of dietary needs, there are also vegetarian, vegan, and gluten-free options. Located in a cooperatively owned building, the cozy café is open for dinner on Wednesday through Friday, with a delightful brunch available on Saturday.

It is the owner's priority to source ingredients and market products from ethical and sustainable sources, buying locally whenever possible. Lara-Bregatta is working to build a strong, lasting relationship with both the vendors and residents of the community. With its affordably delicious mix of ethnic foods, this Dominican-fusion spot has become a popular fixture in its Burlington neighborhood.

In 2022, Café Mamajuana was selected as a semifinalist for a James Beard Foundation Award in the Best New Restaurant Category. After receiving this prestigious honor, Lara-Bregatta now plans to pursue her dream of writing a cookbook. There is no doubt that this latest venture will be a success—for this talented chef and businesswoman all things are possible!

Cotija Salsa

MAKES 2½ CUPS

Aji Amarillo paste is a staple ingredient in Peruvian cuisine. It is made from yellow hot peppers grown in the Andes. It can be found in Latin markets or ordered online. This vibrant versatile sauce has a spicy kick. If you want a less spicy salsa, use ½ tablespoon of the Aji-Amarillo paste. Use this creamy, herbal salsa with a bite as an easy dip for veggies or spoon over chicken, steaks, and fish.

1 small green bell pepper, stemmed, seeded, and coarsely chopped

¼ cup chopped Spanish onion

¼ cup chopped red onion

4 medium garlic cloves, peeled and smashed

1 cup fresh mint leaves, loosely packed, coarsely chopped

1 cup fresh cilantro leaves, loosely packed, coarsely chopped

3 ounces crumbled fresh Cotija cheese

4 tablespoons fresh lime juice, plus more as needed

2 tablespoons fresh lemon juice

1 to 1½ tablespoons Aji-Amarillo paste, or to taste

¾ cup mayonnaise, homemade or store-bought

⅛ teaspoon adobo, plus more for garnish

⅛ teaspoon freshly ground black pepper, or to taste

Kosher salt

Minced cilantro for garnish

1. Place the pepper, onions, garlic, mint, and cilantro leaves into the bowl of a food processor and pulse until vegetables are chopped fine.

2. Add the cheese, lime and lemon juices, and 1 tablespoon of the Aji-Amarillo paste then process until smooth, adjusting the heat with additional Aji-Amarillo paste, if desired. Add the mayonnaise, adobo powder, and pepper and blend on high until slightly grainy in texture, scraping down the sides of the bowl as needed, about 2 minutes. Adjust seasonings with adobo powder, salt, and pepper, to taste. Cover and refrigerate overnight; this will help to firm up the salsa and to meld the flavors. Garnish with cilantro and adobo. Serve with a simple crudité platter.

Note: The sauce can be stored in an airtight container in the refrigerator for up to 5 days. If you can't find fresh Cotija cheese, feta cheese is a great substitute.

Café Mamajuana

DRINKS

DAILY CHOCOLATE

Daily Chocolate is a small-batch chocolate shop located in the heart of Vermont's oldest and smallest city, Vergennes. Nestled in a historic brick building on Green Street, Daily Chocolate hosts a dazzling display of handcrafted chocolates—wine-poached cherry clusters, sea-salted black rum caramels, English toffee, more than a dozen flavors of bark, and honey sponge, made from their very own backyard honey. Owner Dawn Wagner kept the ideas fresh, the flavors inventive, and the look beautiful, all while remaining committed to making ethical and sustainable decisions that not only keep our planet healthy but help support the vast network of farmers and food producers in Vermont.

Daily Chocolate's Hot Cocoa Mix

MAKES ABOUT 16 SERVINGS

This recipe makes a great inexpensive gift. Just scoop the cocoa mixture into an attractive container and tie with a decorative ribbon. Be sure to attach the Hot Cocoa recipe directions (step 2) below. See photo on page 174.

8 ounces dark chocolate (at least 70 percent cacao), coarsely chopped

¾ cup granulated sugar

1⅓ cups unsweetened natural cocoa powder, preferably organic

Pinch kosher salt

1. Process the chocolate in a food processor until finely ground. Add the sugar, cocoa powder, and salt and process until well combined.

2. For each serving, heat 1 cup milk until hot, but not boiling. Add 2 to 4 tablespoons cocoa mix, stirring until the chocolate is melted and smooth. Top with a dollop of whipped cream, chocolate shavings, or marshmallows, if desired.

Note: Store the mixture in an airtight container.

Daily Chocolate

SUNSHINE VALLEY BERRY FARM

In 2007, Rob Meadows and Patricia Rydle were open to a change in career and were considering what business they could do together. When Blair's Berry Farm in Rochester went up for sale, it felt exactly right. They decided that growing berries would be a good fit and purchased the farm, renaming it Sunshine Valley Berry Farm. Today, they cultivate certified organic raspberries and blueberries and sell them from the farm store prepicked or pick-your-own. Over the years, they have attracted a fan base for their jams, as well as for many types of raw honey, some from the farm's hive and others from locations around Vermont.

Sunshine Smoothies

SERVES 4

These smoothies are best enjoyed right away; however, leftovers can be refrigerated for up to three days. If refrigerating, leave as little air at the top of the container as possible to reduce oxidation. You can also freeze this mixture. Add a little lemon or orange juice to the thawed smoothie before serving, to give it a fresh flavor.

1 large handful dandelion greens and flowers, stems removed and discarded

1½ pints blueberries

1 cup spring water, plus extra as needed

¾ cup fresh orange juice

¼ cup fresh lemon juice

¾ cup chopped mango

½ cup baby spinach

2 Medjool dates, pitted

1 tablespoon packed fresh mint leaves, plus extra for garnish

1 tablespoon shredded unsweetened coconut

1 tablespoon plain yogurt (optional)

1½ teaspoons hulled hemp seed or maca powder (optional)

1. Soak the dandelion greens in a large bowl of cold water for about 30 minutes. Rinse and drain the greens; transfer to a blender.

2. Add the blueberries, water, orange juice, lemon juice, mango, spinach, dates, mint, coconut, yogurt, if using, and hemp seed, if using. Blend until smooth, adding extra water if needed. Serve, garnished with mint leaves.

Sunshine Valley Berry Farm

Berry Good Smoothies

SERVES 4

River Berry Farm is a family-owned organic fruit and vegetable farm located on the Lamoille River in Fairfax. The small farm has been in operation since 1992. The owners, Jane and David Marchant, along with a hardworking crew grow crew 50 acres of vegetables, 3 acres of strawberries and 1.5 acres of raspberries. The farm also consists of 21,000 square feet of greenhouse crops. This recipe utilizes the strawberries and raspberries from the farm.

1 cup frozen strawberries, coarsely chopped

¾ cup frozen raspberries or blackberries

2 cups skim milk or soy milk

½ cup plain or vanilla nonfat yogurt

2 tablespoons Vermont honey

Crushed ice (optional)

Place the strawberries, raspberries, milk, yogurt, and honey in a blender and purée until smooth. Divide the mixture among four tall glasses, add crushed ice, if desired, and serve.

River Berry Farm

BHAKTA Sidecar

MAKES 1 COCKTAIL

This classic cocktail is refreshingly tart with hints of sweetness from the orange liqueur and sugar on the rim. Its simple yet sophisticated and can be made with five ingredients.

Rimming sugar as needed

2 ounces brandy, such as **BHAKTA 27-07**

¾ ounce French orange liqueur, such as Cointreau

¾ ounce fresh lemon juice

Orange twist or apple slices for garnish

1. Coat the rim of a coupe glass with rimming sugar, if desired, and set aside.

2. Add the brandy, orange liqueur, and lemon juice to a shaker with ice and shake until well chilled.

3. Strain into the prepared glass.

4. Garnish with an orange twist or thinly sliced apples.

Chef Philip Davis for BHAKTA 50 Spirits

APPALACHIAN GAP DISTILLERY

The founders of the Appalachian Gap Distillery in Middlebury, Vermont, began their business venture in 2010. Founders Lars Hubbard and Chuck Burkins started with a property that needed to be completely renovated. Over the next three years, they readied the building for production. The two men were involved with every aspect of the design and construction of the original space, including the addition of a tasting room.

The artisanal distillery sits at the foot of the Green Mountains (part of the Appalachian chain) in Middlebury, Vermont. All the electricity for the building is generated by solar power and its boilers are fueled by renewable natural gas. The distillery has been certified by Climate Neutral, a non-profit that works with brands to decrease global greenhouse gas emissions. This certification means that the Appalachian Gap Distillery takes responsibility for its carbon emissions and is helping to reduce its carbon footprint.

Appalachian Gap Distillery's spirits are not made in bulk but are instead crafted to meet the company's exacting standards. This means that the spirits are unique, rich in flavor and well-balanced. They capture the essence of Vermont by using local ingredients and flavor. The end-product is Drumlin Rye, Ridgeline Whiskey, Mythic Gin, Peregrine Gin, Split Spirits, and Papilio (a Vermonter's take on Tequila).

Every person who works at the distillery, including founders and employees, as well as tasting room and event staff, must work on every part of the process—from mashing to distilling, to bottling and shipping. This hands-on approach enables participants to know exactly what goes into each and every bottle. Appalachian Gap Distillery's motto is "Small Batch from Scratch."

Mythic Basil Transition

MAKES 1 COCKTAIL

"We wanted a botanical gin that expressed the bounty of Vermont, enhanced with flavors that are rarely, if ever, used in gin. Our base spirit is the same as is used for all of our grain-based spirits, distilled to a much higher proof to create a neutral base. Balsam fir needles, rose hips, lemon peel, and even chamomile and Szechuan peppercorns (along with a number of other botanicals), are macerated with the traditional juniper berries, then redistilled with our small pot still to create an intensely flavored herbal experience with a beautiful nose and round mouthfeel," says Appalachian Gap Distillery.

2 basil leaves plus 1 extra leaf for garnish

1½ ounces Appalachian Gap Mythic Gin

½ ounce St Germain Elderflower Liqueur

¾ ounce fresh lemon juice

½ ounce simple syrup, or to taste

1. Chill one wine glass in the refrigerator.

2. Using a cocktail muddler or a spoon, gently mash the basil leaves in empty cocktail shaker. Combine the gin, elderflower liqueur, lemon juice, and simple syrup in a shaker three-quarters filled with ice. Vigorously shake for about 30 seconds.

3. Strain into the chilled glass, then add some ice. Garnish with basil leaf. Serve at once with a reusable shatter resistant clear glass straw.

Appalachian Gap Distillery

Drumlin Whiskey Sour

MAKES 1 COCKTAIL

"Our Drumlin Rye is the perfect expression of the terroir of our warm and fertile valley. Every bit of rye in the spirit is grown within 25 miles of the distillery, and we use rye and *only* rye to create a rich, peppery, complex spirit. We start with a mash of 100-percent rye—no barley, no other grains—which we know is a little extra work but results in stronger, more vibrant flavor. Double distilled, it is then aged in new American oak barrels for at least three years. We make just a dozen barrels a year," says Appalachian Gap Distillery.

2 ounces Drumlin Rye

¾ ounce fresh lemon juice

½ ounce Vermont maple syrup

1 large organic egg white

2 to 4 drops Angostura bitters, or to taste

1. Chill 1 coup glass in the refrigerator.

2. Add the whiskey, lemon juice, maple syrup, and the egg white to a cocktail shaker, and dry shake (without ice) for 30 seconds. Add ice to the shaker and vigorously shake for another 30 seconds.

3. Strain into a chilled coupe and top with bitters. Serve at once.

Appalachian Gap Distillery

Papilio Paloma

MAKES 1 COCKTAIL

"We taste a smokiness in Vermont's own dark maple syrup that we thought would pair well with the smokiness of agave spirits, like tequila. Rather than adding maple syrup to a base spirit, making it sweet, we fermented agave syrup and maple syrup together to create an utterly unique 'Vtquila.' We import organic blue agave nectar from Jalisco, Mexico, and mix it 4:1 with dark maple syrup. Three to four weeks of fermentation and double distillation through our hybrid still result in a spirit like no other in the world," says Appalachian Gap Distillery.

2 ounces Appalachian Gap Distillery Papilio

4 ounces grapefruit soda, or as needed

½ ounce fresh lime juice

Vermont maple syrup as needed

1 grapefruit peel for garnish

1 dehydrated lemon wheel for garnish

1. Chill 1 glass in the refrigerator.

2. Fill the chilled glass with some ice. Add the Papilio, grapefruit soda, and lime juice, stirring with a bar spoon until well combined. Adjust sweetness with maple syrup, if desired.

3. Garnish with grapefruit peel and dehydrated lemon wheel. Serve at once with a copper straw.

Appalachian Gap Distillery

Ridgeline Boulevardier

MAKES 1 COCKTAIL

"We imagined Ridgeline before we even started up our distillery—a rich whiskey, reminiscent of bourbon and Irish whiskies, but with a character all its own. We start with a mash of local barley, corn, and rye. Double distilled, it is then aged in new American oak barrels and finished in port wine barrels to create a truly special whiskey," says Appalachian Gap Distillery.

2 ounces Appalachian Gap Ridgeline Vermont Whiskey

¾ ounce bitter aperitivo liqueur, such as Campari

¾ ounce sweet vermouth, such as Carpano Antica

Orange peel for garnish

1. Combine all the ingredients in a shaker three-quarters filled with ice. Vigorously shake for about 30 seconds.

2. Strain into a rock glass or decorative glass. Garnish with an orange peel. Serve at once.

Appalachian Gap Distillery

DESSERTS

Maple Roast Pumpkin Pie

SERVES 8

It had never occurred to Claire Georges, the owner of Butterfly Bakery, to use fresh pumpkin in baked goods when canned was so widely used, but a few years ago, a friend of hers received a pumpkin from her CSA. They stared at the gourd-like squash for a while and then decided to give pie a try before the pumpkin went bad (with little hope for success). The results were amazing. Georges has never gone back to using canned pumpkin for anything since.

This recipe produces more purée than you will need for the pie. You can store the remaining pumpkin purée in an airtight container in the refrigerator for up to five days or in the freezer for several months. In a pinch, you can substitute 1½ cups of organic canned purée (just be sure not to use pie filling, which is spiced and sweetened). Serve the pie with vanilla or maple ice cream, or a dollop of whipped cream. See photo on page 184.

1 pie pumpkin (3 to 4 pounds)

3 large eggs, lightly beaten

⅔ cup pure Vermont maple syrup

1½ teaspoons vanilla extract

1 teaspoon ground cinnamon

½ teaspoon ground ginger

¼ teaspoon ground cloves

1 (9-inch) unbaked pie shell

1. Preheat the oven to 450°F. Lightly grease a baking sheet and set aside.

2. Cut the pumpkin in half lengthwise; scoop out the seeds and strings and discard them. Place the pumpkin, open side down, on the prepared baking sheet. Roast until fork-tender, about 40 minutes. Set aside to cool. When the pumpkin is cool enough to handle, scoop out the flesh, transfer to a food processor, and process until smooth.

3. Reduce the oven temperature to 350°F. In a large bowl, whisk together 1½ cups of the pumpkin purée, the eggs, maple syrup, vanilla, cinnamon, ginger, and cloves until smooth. Pour the mixture into the pie shell and bake for 30 minutes. Rotate the pie and bake, until a knife inserted into the center comes out clean, about 30 minutes. Let cool slightly; serve warm or at room temperature.

Claire Georges of Butterfly Bakery for
the Capital City Farmers Market

CAPITAL CITY FARMERS MARKET

As one of the oldest farmers' markets in Vermont, the Capital City Farmers Market in Montpelier offers customers a wide variety of fresh fruits and vegetables, cheeses, meats, honey, maple syrup, spirits, wild edibles, plants, and cut flowers, as well as prepared foods and crafts—every season, all year long. To highlight and promote the region's local farms, the market requires that all food vendors use at least three local farm ingredients in their products and post signs listing the farms that their ingredients came from.

Customers can learn how to use the fresh foods they buy from the market's farmers at the many demonstrations hosted during the year, which are in partnership with local chefs and the New England Culinary Institute. With 52 vendors at its outdoor market, and over 30 at its indoor location, there's always something new and exciting to try at the market.

SAXTON'S RIVER DISTILLERY

Part of Christian Stromberg's Lithuanian heritage is making a traditional spiced honey liqueur called Krupnikas, which is typically served at weddings and other celebrations. Making Krupnikas opened the door for Stromberg to create other liqueurs, and living in Vermont led him to experiment with maple syrup. Beginning on the banks of the Saxtons River in Cambridgeport, Vermont, in 2006 and in a lightly heated barn, Stromberg developed unique maple liqueurs, bourbons, and ryes. After moving to Brattleboro in 2011, he further developed an award-winning gin and a coffee liqueur made from locally roasted coffee. The company continues to grow, gaining new fans as they are introduced to unique products with European roots and a distinctly Vermont character.

Sapling Tiramisu

SERVES 6 TO 8

This tiramisu recipe has been in Christian Stromberg's mother-in-law's recipe file for three decades. The original recipe uses Marsala, but Stromberg makes it with Sapling Vermont Maple Liqueur. The liqueur has a lovely maple flavor, which is excellent for tiramisu because it complements the smooth and creamy custard-like layers of the dish. Stromberg uses mascarpone cheese from Vermont Creamery in this dessert.

4 large eggs, separated

½ cup granulated sugar

1 (16-ounce) container mascarpone cheese

⅛ teaspoon salt

1 cup heavy cream, chilled

2 cups very strong brewed coffee or espresso, cooled

2–4 tablespoons Sapling Vermont
    or other maple liqueur

2 boxes (24 per box) traditional Savoiardi
    ladyfingers, approx. 48 biscuits

Unsweetened cocoa powder or
    shaved dark chocolate

1. Lightly grease a 9 x 13-inch baking dish and set aside.

2. Using an electric mixture, beat together the egg yolks and 6 tablespoons of the sugar until thick, about 4 minutes. Add the mascarpone and beat until smooth. In a separate bowl, beat together the egg whites and salt until soft peaks form. In a third bowl, beat together the heavy cream and remaining 2 tablespoons sugar until soft peaks form. Fold the cream into the mascarpone mixture and then fold in the beaten egg whites.

3. Combine the coffee and maple liqueur in a shallow bowl. Quickly dip each ladyfinger in the coffee mixture, soaking for 2 to 3 seconds, and arrange half of them in the prepared baking dish. Spread half of the mascarpone mixture evenly over the top. Repeat with the remaining ladyfingers and mascarpone mixture.

4. Cover the tiramisu with plastic wrap and refrigerate for at least 8 hours. Just before serving, dust with cocoa powder or shaved dark chocolate.

Saxton's River Distillery

OSBORNE FAMILY MAPLE

Osborne Family Maple, in the remote Northeast Kingdom town of Ferdinand, where moose outnumber people three to one, dates back to the late 1930s. Four generations of Osbornes have patiently managed the land, resulting in the 4,000-tap sugarbush that they have today. Certified organic maple producers, the Osborne family manages their woods to promote biodiversity as well as sap production, because a healthy forest ecosystem is much less susceptible to nonnative pests and invasive plants. They approach their recipes in much the same way, using fresh, local ingredients and pure Vermont maple syrup to bring new life to traditional recipes.

Maple Bars

MAKES 16 BARS

These chewy, sweet bars are a treat served on their own or with maple or vanilla ice cream.

Crust

1 cup plus 1 tablespoon all-purpose flour

⅓ cup packed light brown sugar

8 tablespoons (4 ounces) butter

Maple Filling

1 cup pure Vermont maple syrup

¾ cup packed light brown sugar

3 large eggs, lightly beaten

2 tablespoons all-purpose flour

½ teaspoon vanilla extract

1½ cups unsweetened shredded coconut

½ cup chopped pecans

1. To make the crust: Preheat the oven to 425°F. Place the flour and sugar in a medium bowl. Blend in the butter using a pastry cutter or your fingers, until the mixture begins to form pea-sized pieces. Press into a 9-inch square baking pan. Bake for 5 minutes.

2. To make the maple filling: Meanwhile, stir the maple syrup and sugar together in a medium saucepan over medium heat until the sugar has dissolved. Let cool, then whisk in the eggs, flour, and vanilla. Stir in the coconut. Pour the filling over the crust and sprinkle the pecans evenly over the top.

3. Bake for 10 minutes, then reduce the heat to 350°F and continue to bake until golden brown, about 20 minutes longer. Let cool in the pan for 15 minutes before cutting.

Osborne Family Maple

SCOTT FARM

The Scott Farm Dummerston has a recorded history dating back to 1791, when George Washington was serving his first term as president. The farm consists of 571 acres and 23 buildings, all of which are listed on the National Register of Historic Places. When the Landmark Trust USA, a Vermont nonprofit, took over the farm in 1995, many of the buildings had fallen into disrepair and the orchard was growing a single variety of apple. This apple, McIntosh, was conventionally sprayed and sold on the wholesale market. The trust, with the help of many hands at Scott Farm, transformed the orchard into one that now contains over 130 varieties of apples, all ecologically grown and marketed both locally and regionally. The farm also grows peaches, plums, nectarines, pears, berries, grapes, cherries, and hard-to-find fruits such as quince, medlars, and gooseberries. The Scott Farm's buildings have been thoughtfully repaired and upgraded so that they are beautifully preserved and energy-efficient. The farm hosts educational programs, workshops, and weddings. Two of its historic houses have been authentically restored and are available for short-term holiday rental.

Applesauce Cake

SERVES 12 TO 15

Although you can use store-bought applesauce for this cake, homemade makes it really special. Scott Farm uses a combination of Bramley's Seedling, Reine des Reinettes, Rhode Island Greening, Ribston Pippin and Sheep's Nose in their applesauce. If you can't find those varieties, any of these would make a lovely applesauce: McIntosh, Cortland, Red Astrakan, Gala, Gravenstein, or Paula Red.

2 cups all-purpose flour

1 cup granulated sugar

1 teaspoon salt

1½ teaspoons baking powder

¾ teaspoon baking soda

½ teaspoon ground cinnamon

⅛ teaspoon ground cloves

⅛ teaspoon grated nutmeg

2 large eggs

4 tablespoons (2 ounces) unsalted butter, softened

2 cups applesauce, preferably homemade

½ teaspoon vanilla extract

Confectioners' sugar

1. Preheat the oven to 375°F. Spray a 9 x 13-inch baking pan with nonstick cooking spray and set aside. Sift together the flour, sugar, salt, baking powder, baking soda, cinnamon, cloves, and nutmeg.

2. Using an electric mixer, beat together the eggs, butter, applesauce, and vanilla until smooth. Fold in the flour mixture until just combined, being careful not to overmix.

3. Pour the batter into the pan and spread evenly. Bake until a toothpick inserted into the center comes out clean, about 25 minutes. Set the cake pan on a cooling rack and let cool completely. Cut into squares, dust with confectioners' sugar, and serve.

Scott Farm

Country Apple Cake

SERVES 6 TO 8

Apples can have an amazing variety of colors, textures, shapes, and tastes. And sometimes the best thing you can do with an apple recipe is to let the fruit speak for itself. This recipe for apple cake is a delicious example. For the best flavor, use a few varieties of apple in this cake. Good choices include the French heirlooms Calville Blanc d'Hiver, a 15th-century apple that has a vanilla-like flavor and a wonderful texture when cooked, and Reine des Reinettes, a juicy apple from the 1700s that has a high sugar content balanced with acidity. This moist, dense light caramel color cake is great served as a dessert with ice cream or as a quick breakfast treat.

3 cups all-purpose flour

1 tablespoon baking powder

1 teaspoon ground cinnamon

½ teaspoon salt

1 cup vegetable oil

2 cups granulated sugar

4 large eggs

2½ teaspoons vanilla extract

4 apples, cored and chopped into 1-inch pieces

1. Center a rack in the oven and preheat to 350°F. Spray a 12-cup Bundt or tube pan with nonstick cooking spray and set aside. In a large bowl sift together the flour, baking powder, cinnamon, and salt.

2. Using an electric mixer, cream together the oil, sugar, eggs, and vanilla, scraping down the sides of the bowl as needed. Add the flour mixture and beat until smooth.

3. Pour half of the batter into the prepared pan and layer half of the apples on top. Repeat with the remaining batter and apples. Bake until a toothpick inserted in the center of the cake comes out clean, about 1¼ hours.

4. Let the cake cool in the pan for about 15 minutes, then invert onto a cooling rack and let cool completely. Reinvert onto a serving plate and serve.

Kelly Carlin for Scott Farm

Chocolate Zucchini Cake

MAKES 15 TO 20 PIECES

This cake recipe, courtesy of Hillary and Gaelan Chutter-Ames, is a great way to use that extra mid-summer zucchini. The zucchini keeps the cake nice and moist. It is a sure hit for coffee breaks and a terrific snack for children, who will never suspect that it contains vegetables.

2½ cups all-purpose flour

¼ cup unsweetened cocoa

1 teaspoon baking soda

½ teaspoon baking powder

½ teaspoon ground cinnamon

½ teaspoon ground cloves

8 tablespoons (4 ounces) unsalted butter, softened

1¾ cups granulated sugar

½ cup vegetable or canola oil

½ cup buttermilk

2 large eggs, lightly beaten

1 teaspoon vanilla extract

2¼ cups packed, grated zucchini

⅓ cup chocolate chips

1. Preheat the oven to 325°F. Spray a 9 x 13-inch pan with nonstick cooking spray and set aside. Whisk together the flour, cocoa, baking soda, baking powder, cinnamon, and cloves.

2. Using an electric mixer, beat the butter, sugar, oil, buttermilk, eggs, and vanilla for 3 minutes, scraping down the sides of the bowl as needed. Add the flour mixture and beat until smooth. Fold in the zucchini and pour the batter into the prepared pan.

3. Sprinkle the chocolate chips evenly over the top. Bake the cake until a toothpick inserted in the center comes out clean, 45 to 50 minutes.

4. Let the cake cool in the pan for 15 minutes, then invert onto a cooling rack and let cool completely before serving.

Hillary and Gaelan Chutter-Ames for Pomykala Farm

THE BAKERY AT THE FARMHOUSE KITCHEN

Located in Burlington, the Bakery at the Farmhouse Kitchen is the home of the original buttercrunch cake. Emily Conn, the bakery's owner, models these buttery, moist cakes with their nice contrasting buttercrunch topping after an old family recipe. The idea for an almond buttercrunch cake–centric bakery originated when Conn's family and friends continuously requested (and, at times, begged for) the cake, which was the highlight of many special occasions and celebrations. The flavor of the cake varies and is adaptable to Vermont's seasonal bounty.

Winter Pudding with Caramelized Cranberries

SERVES 8

This recipe makes more cranberry sauce than you will need in the cake; save the extra cranberries and serve over ice cream or pancakes. Be sure not to overmix the batter in step 3 or the pudding will not rise as much. In the summer, this recipe works well with sour cherries.

2 cups granulated sugar

2 tablespoons water

3 cups fresh cranberries

8 tablespoons (4 ounces) unsalted butter

¾ cup all-purpose flour

2 teaspoons baking powder

Pinch salt

¾ cup milk

½ teaspoon vanilla extract

1. Preheat the oven to 350°F.

2. Combine 1 cup of the sugar and the water in a medium skillet over medium-low heat and stir until the sugar begins to dissolve. Add the cranberries and continue to cook, stirring often, until they soften and begin to pop, about 10 minutes. Set aside.

3. Melt the butter in a 10-inch cast-iron skillet in the oven. Sift the remaining 1 cup sugar, the flour, baking powder, and salt into a medium bowl. Add the milk and vanilla, stirring until almost combined. Do not overmix.

4. When the butter has melted, carefully remove the pan from the oven. Pour the batter into the middle of the pan. As you pour, quickly tilt the pan in all directions to spread the batter evenly across the bottom of the pan. Pour 2 cups of the cranberries in the middle of the dough. Do not mix the berries into the batter. Carefully return the pan to the oven and bake until the fruit starts to bubble and the edges are nicely browned, 45 minutes to 1 hour. Let cool slightly, then serve.

The Bakery at the Farmhouse Kitchen

No-Bake Vanilla Bean Cheesecake

SERVES 6

This rich cheesecake is both simple and delicious. It has no crust, requires no baking, and the vanilla bean imbues it with a luscious flavor. Angela loves this recipe so much that she used to sell the little cheesecakes at the West River Farmers' Market in Londonderry. It is inspired by a no-bake cheesecake in *Instant Gratification,* by Lauren Chattman, which is Angela's bible for simple, quick desserts. Angela uses Mettowee cheese, a fresh, creamy, pasteurized goat's milk chèvre named for the Mettowee River Valley, in this cheesecake, but you can substitute another mild, fresh goat cheese, or cream cheese. For a delightful topping, slice some berries or stone fruit, such as peaches or plums, and soak them in a bit of sugar.

½ teaspoon unflavored gelatin

2 tablespoons water

½ vanilla bean

1 pound Mettowee cheese

6 tablespoons heavy cream

⅔ cup granulated sugar

1. Spray a 6-inch springform pan with nonstick cooking spray and set aside. Place the gelatin in a small heatproof bowl. Add the water and mix until well combined; let stand for 3 minutes.

2. Meanwhile, pour 1 inch of water into a small saucepan and bring to a simmer over medium heat. Place the bowl with the gelatin over (but not touching) the simmering water and stir just until the gelatin is completely dissolved, about 2 minutes (do not overheat the gelatin). Let cool.

3. Place the vanilla bean on a work surface and split it in half lengthwise using a paring knife. Scrape the seeds into a large bowl and add the Mettowee, heavy cream, and sugar.

4. Using an electric mixer, beat the cheese mixture until light and fluffy, about 3 minutes, scraping down the sides of the bowl as needed. Beat in the gelatin mixture until well blended, scraping down the bowl. Scrape the batter into the springform pan and smooth the top with a rubber spatula. Cover with plastic wrap and refrigerate until firm, 6 hours or overnight.

5. To unmold, run a hot knife around the edge of the pan to loosen, and gently release the sides of the pan. Set the cake, supported by the springform base, on a cake plate and serve. (The cheesecake will keep, covered and refrigerated, up to four days.)

Angela Miller of Consider Bardwell Farm

VERMONT SPIRITS

The team at Vermont Spirits passionately hand-makes each distinctive, award-winning spirit in small batches, on custom-designed copper and glass stills. The Meeting House at the Distillery features a curated tasting experience and an opportunity for the local community and its visitors to come together in good company.

Made from the highest-quality, locally sourced ingredients, Vermont Spirits are crafted with a passion for heritage, craftsmanship, and a keen stewardship of the land. Their production is one-of-a-kind, featuring five uniquely customized stills. Most impressive, and at the heart of their distillery operation, are the gorgeous 24-foot-tall glass fractioning column stills, custom designed and built for Vermont Gold Vodka. But not to be outdone, the pot still was converted from a local chocolatier's copper pot, and the stripping still is made out of a recycled maple arch from a nearby maple farm. No. 14 Bourbon and Coppers Barrel Gin are barreled, tasted, blended, and aged in the distillery.

Vermont Spirits is committed to the kind of craftsmanship that is difficult to find today. Spirits are distilled, cut and blended entirely by sight, sound, and taste, without the use of proofs or set points. The process of making craft spirits is actually quite simple but requires the caring attention

of the master distiller to monitor each batch from start to finish. The team at Vermont Spirits is constantly tasting and adjusting their blends to make the best-tasting, most-consistent spirits possible.

While the artisan craft relies on creative problem solving, the quality of Vermont Spirits products is defined by the ingredients. Pure Vermont water, locally handpicked juniper, and maple syrup sourced from local community farms are the backbone of their high-quality spirits.

Vermont Spirits uses the ingenuity of its team to source responsibly, reuse, and recycle. From repurposed equipment, to fertilizing the nearby lawn with the distillery's stripping waste, it is committed to sustainable operations. In fact, the distillery aims to be a carbon-neutral distillery in the near future.

Vermont Spirited Apple Ice Cream

MAKES 1 QUART

This recipe takes a bit of advance planning; make both the apple mixture and ice cream mixture the day before you plan to serve the ice cream.

Vermont Spirited Apples

3 cups peeled, cored, and diced Granny Smith apples (3 large or 4 medium apples)

½ cup vodka

2 tablespoons pure Vermont maple syrup

Pinch ground cinnamon

Pinch salt

Ice Cream

2 cups whole milk

3 large eggs

½ cup plus 1 tablespoon pure Vermont maple syrup

3 tablespoons sugar

2 cups heavy cream

1. To make the Vermont Spirited Apples: Preheat the oven to 350°F. Butter a 1-quart casserole dish, then add the apples, 2 tablespoons of the vodka, the maple syrup, cinnamon, and salt. Stir to combine. Cover the casserole dish and bake until the apples are very tender, 30 to 35 minutes. Let cool to room temperature, then add the remaining 6 tablespoons vodka and refrigerate overnight.

2. To make the ice cream: Beat the milk and eggs together in a large saucepan. Add the maple syrup and sugar. Cook over low heat, stirring constantly, until the mixture is thickened and coats a wooden spoon, about 10 minutes. (The mixture should be just beginning to boil.) Let cool and then stir in the heavy cream. Refrigerate overnight.

3. Pour the ice cream mixture into an ice cream machine and freeze according to the manufacturer's directions. When the batter is nearly frozen, add the apple mixture and continue processing until thoroughly mixed and firm. Transfer the ice cream to a container and freeze.

Edward F. Nesta and Debra C. Argen of Luxury Experience for Vermont Spirits

Luxury Experience's Apple Pie with Tipsy Raisins

SERVES 8

The raisins need to soak in vodka overnight, so be sure to start this step the day before you plan to serve the pie. You can enjoy this apple pie on its own or, for a decadent treat, serve it on a pool of Maple Sauce (recipe follows) and top it with a scoop of Vermont Spirited Apple Ice Cream (page 198).

Pie Filling

¼ cup raisins

2 tablespoons vodka

4 Granny Smith apples, cored, peeled, and sliced

3 tablespoons pure Vermont maple syrup

Pastry

2½ cups unbleached all-purpose flour

2 tablespoons granulated sugar

1 teaspoon salt

12 tablespoons (6 ounces) unsalted
    butter, cut into cubes and chilled

½ cup vegetable shortening, cut
    into cubes and chilled

6–8 tablespoons vodka, chilled

Cinnamon sugar, for sprinkling the pastry leaves

1. To make the filling: Place the raisins and vodka in a jar. Put the lid on the jar and shake to coat the raisins with the vodka. Let sit for several hours or overnight.

2. Preheat the oven to 350°F. Toss the apples with the maple syrup and raisins and set aside.

3. To make the pastry: Process the flour, sugar, and salt in a food processor to blend. Add the butter and shortening, a few pieces at a time, and pulse just to combine. Add 6 tablespoons of the chilled vodka and pulse until the dough starts to hold together. If the dough is too crumbly, add the remaining 2 tablespoons vodka as needed. Do not overprocess.

4. Divide the dough in half and roll one half out between sheets of parchment paper to form a 12-inch round. Carefully transfer the dough to a 9-inch pie plate, spoon the filling into the crust, and smooth the top. Roll the remaining dough into a 12-inch round and place on the filling. Trim any excess dough from the crusts and then crimp together to seal.

5. Roll the leftover dough out ⅛ inch thick and use a leaf cookie cutter to cut shapes from it. Place the leaves on a baking sheet and sprinkle them with cinnamon sugar. Bake pie and pastry leaves until golden brown: about 12 minutes for the leaves, 35 to 40 minutes for the pies. Let the pie cool slightly, then serve with the pastry leaves.

Edward F. Nesta and Debra C. Argen of Luxury Experience for Vermont Spirits

MAPLE SAUCE

MAKES 1 CUP

½ cup sweetened condensed milk

½ cup pure Vermont maple syrup

Stir together the milk and maple syrup in a microwave-safe bowl. Microwave for 1 minute; watch carefully so the mixture does not boil over. Let cool slightly before serving.

Edward F. Nesta and Debra C. Argen of Luxury Experience for Vermont Spirits

Bayley Hazen Blue Cheesecake with Hazelnut Crust and Poached Pears

SERVES 12

This cheesecake was inspired by the incredible variety of artisan cheeses made in Vermont. Jasper Hill Farm's Bayley Hazen Blue was chosen for its slightly crumbly, dense texture and balanced, nutty flavor. A blue cheese cheesecake isn't your typical restaurant fare, nor is it something you might think to make at home, but it is well worth trying. The hazelnuts and pears complement the blue cheese filling perfectly. This makes an unusual savory dessert or, cut into smaller portions, an elegant appetizer.

Cheesecake

1 cup ground hazelnuts

1 cup graham cracker crumbs

4 tablespoons (2 ounces) unsalted butter, melted

12 ounces cream cheese, softened

12 ounces Bayley Hazen Blue cheese, room temperature

4 large eggs, lightly beaten

1 cup heavy cream

¼ cup Worcestershire sauce

2 tablespoons Tabasco sauce

½ teaspoon salt

2 teaspoons freshly ground black pepper

Poached Pears

2 cups port wine

2 tablespoons granulated sugar

2 firm Bartlett or Bosc pears, peeled, cored, and quartered

1. To make the cheesecake: Preheat the oven to 350°F. Stir together the hazelnuts, graham cracker crumbs, and butter. Press gently into the bottom of a 9-inch springform pan. Set aside.

2. With an electric mixer, beat together the cream cheese, blue cheese, eggs, cream, Worcestershire sauce, Tabasco sauce, salt, and pepper until smooth, scraping down the sides of the bowl as needed. Spread the cheese filling evenly over the crust and smooth the top with a rubber spatula. Set the springform pan in a roasting pan and add enough hot water to come halfway up the sides of the springform pan. Bake for 50 minutes. Remove from the water bath and let cool to room temperature, then cover with plastic wrap and refrigerate for 8 hours or overnight.

3. To make the poached pears: Combine the port wine and sugar in a medium saucepan and bring to a boil over medium-high heat. Reduce the heat to medium-low, add the pears, cover, and cook until the pears are tender, 12 to 15 minutes. Transfer the pears to a plate and refrigerate. Increase the heat to medium-high and reduce the poaching liquid by half, about 10 minutes. Pour the liquid into a heatproof container and refrigerate for at least 30 minutes, or until ready to serve.

4. To unmold the cheesecake, run a hot knife around the edge of the pan to loosen, and gently release the sides of the pan. Set the cake, supported by the springform base, on a cake plate. Slice each pear quarter lengthwise into 3 thin slices and arrange the slices in a circular fan design on top of the cake. Cut the cheesecake into wedges, spoon a little of the reserved poaching liquid around each piece, and serve.

West Mountain Inn

LEDGENEAR FARM

Ledgenear Farm is a hilltop farm and homestead dating back to the 1850s. Hardscrabble but beautiful, the farm has provided for multiple generations by growing field crops, herding sheep, milking cows, and producing maple syrup. Ledgenear Farm has approximately 250 acres of hay fields, pasture, mixed softwoods and maple sugar woods with 2,000 maple taps. James Coe was born on the farm. He and his wife, Nella, have operated their architectural practice from the homestead for the past 10 years. They have expanded the farm to include wool, apple orchards, flower and vegetable greenhouses, agrotourism guesthouses, and pasture-raised beef. Now grown, the next generation of Coes is working and growing the farm with James and Nella.

Maple Apple Pie

SERVES 8

This apple pie recipe has been made countless times at Ledgenear Farm and lovingly shared with family and friends. The Coes think that it is the perfect combination of lemon, maple syrup, and apples. The recipe is a great example of how maple syrup can be used as a sugar substitute in baking. Serve the pie with a dollop of whipped cream or a scoop of maple or vanilla ice cream, if desired.

Crust

2 cups all-purpose flour

2 teaspoons salt

16 tablespoons (8 ounces) unsalted butter

⅓ cup water

1 teaspoon granulated sugar

Filling

8 Cortland or McIntosh apples, peeled, cored, and cut into chunks

1 tablespoon all-purpose flour

¾ cup pure Vermont maple syrup, or to taste

1 teaspoon fresh lemon juice

½ teaspoon ground cinnamon

¼ teaspoon grated nutmeg

Coarse sugar, as needed

1. To make the crust. Preheat the oven to 375°F. Combine the flour, sugar, and salt in a large bowl. With a pastry cutter or your fingers, cut the butter into the flour until the mixture begins to form pea-sized pieces. Add the water, 1 tablespoon at a time, and mix until the dough just comes together. Do not overmix. Turn the dough out onto a lightly floured work surface and form into two disks. Roll one disk into a 12-inch round. Transfer to a 9-inch pie plate and trim the excess dough, leaving ½-inch overhang.

2. To make the filling: Combine the apples and flour in a large bowl. Pour the apples into the crust and drizzle with the maple syrup and lemon juice. Sprinkle the cinnamon and nutmeg over the top.

3. Roll the second disk of dough out to a 12-inch round and place it over the apple filling. Trim the excess dough along the edge, leaving ½-inch overhang. Fold the edges of the dough under, then crimp to seal. Cut slits in the top crust and sprinkle with coarse sugar.

4. Place the pie on a baking sheet and bake until the apples are tender and the filling is bubbling, about 1¼ hours. (If necessary, cover the perimeter of the crust with a foil collar to prevent it from overbrowning.) Transfer the pie to a cooling rack and let cool completely before serving.

Ledgenear Farm

CEDAR CIRCLE FARM & EDUCATION CENTER

Located in East Thetford, Cedar Circle Farm & Education Center is a nonprofit organization dedicated to agricultural education and scientific research in the public interest, in addition to being a working, certified organic vegetable and berry farm. Cedar Circle sits on 40 acres overlooking the Connecticut River and has been conserved by the Vermont Land trust since 1990. In its more than 20 years of existence, the farm has prioritized the involvement of community members as it has developed and shared practices that promote regenerative agriculture, good health, and a resource-rich environment. Cedar Circle is home to a bustling farmstand cafe, commercial kitchen, and education center. It's a place where families, friends, and neighbors gather to learn about organic regenerative agriculture, explore the farm, purchase farm-fresh organic fruits and vegetables, pick-your-own berries, and delight in locally grown organic food.

Butternut Apple Crisp

SERVES 8

At the 2011 Pumpkin Festival the farm was eager to get away from the heavy, cloying desserts most often seen in autumn. The farm's stores were bursting with winter squash and bushels of apples that looked so good side by side, they decided to pair them in this twist on a classic crisp. At the farm, they get their apples from Champlain Orchards, in Shoreham, or from their own trees. This recipe works well if you use a mixture of firm, tart apples, such as Granny Smith, and apples that soften when cooked, such as McIntosh.

Topping

1 cup raw whole almonds

¾ cup all-purpose flour

½ cup packed light brown sugar

½ cup granulated sugar

¾ teaspoon ground cinnamon

½ teaspoon grated nutmeg

12 tablespoons (6 ounces) unsalted butter, cut into ½-inch pieces

Filling

¾ cup granulated sugar

¼ cup packed light brown sugar

Zest and juice from 1 lemon

1 teaspoon vanilla extract

1 teaspoon tapioca starch

1 teaspoon ground cinnamon

½ teaspoon grated nutmeg

½ teaspoon ground ginger

1½ pounds butternut squash (1 small), peeled, seeded and cut into ⅛-inch slices (4 cups)

6 large apples, peeled, cored, and cut into ⅛-inch slices

Vanilla ice cream, for serving

1. To make the topping: Preheat the oven to 200°F. Place the almonds in a single layer on a baking sheet and toast, stirring occasionally, until golden brown, about 40 minutes. Set aside to cool.

2. To make the filling: Increase the oven temperature to 375°F. Lightly grease a 9 x 13-inch baking dish and set aside.

3. Combine the granulated sugar, brown sugar, lemon zest and juice, vanilla, tapioca starch, cinnamon, nutmeg, and ginger in a large bowl. Add the squash and apples and toss to coat. Spoon into prepared baking dish. Cover and bake until the squash is fork-tender, about 30 minutes.

4. Meanwhile, process the almonds in a food processor until coarsely ground. Add the flour, sugars, cinnamon, nutmeg, and salt and pulse to blend. Add the butter and pulse until crumbly.

5. Stir the filling and sprinkle the topping evenly over the top. Bake uncovered until the crisp is light golden brown and bubbling, about 30 minutes.

6. Cool the crisp slightly, allowing the juices to be absorbed, and serve with ice cream, if desired.

Note: If you use a mandoline, preparation for this dish is very quick and easy. Otherwise, slicing up the squash and apples takes some time, but larger pieces will work just as well.

Alison Baker for Cedar Circle Farm

SIMON PEARCE

From growing up in his father's workshop in Ireland to opening a flagship shop, glassblowing studio, and farm-to-table restaurant in Quechee with his wife, Pia, over 40 years ago—Simon's life has always centered around beautiful, functional design and time spent with family.

The Simon Pearce Restaurant + Bar was voted one of America's Most Romantic Restaurants by *Travel and Leisure* and annual recipient of *Wine Spectator*'s "Best of Award of Excellence." A top Vermont tourism destination, visitors come year-round to experience the joy of creativity—and the beauty of a quintessential Vermont setting, which includes a quaint covered bridge and breathtaking views of the rushing Ottauquechee River, which sustainably fuels the turbine-powered glassblowing workshop.

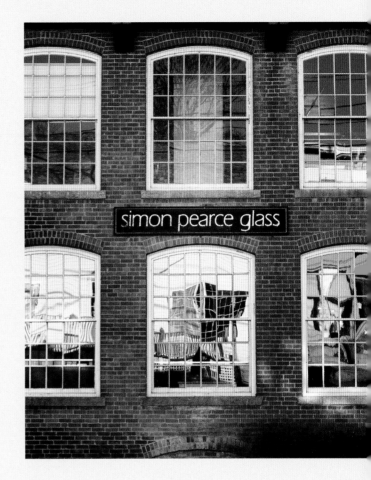

Warm Apple Crisp with Hazelnut Crumble

SERVES 10 TO 12

In autumn look for firm, local, organic apples for this easy recipe. Calvados is a very nice alternative to domestic Applejack. Handmade in their Windsor, Vermont, pottery factory, Simon Pearce's Cavendish Serving Dish is the perfect choice for cooking and serving this flavorful crisp.

Apple Filling

Grated zest and juice of 1 lemon

½ cup Vermont apple cider

½ cup granulated sugar

⅛ teaspoon ground cinnamon

⅛ teaspoon grated nutmeg

4 tablespoons (2 ounces) unsalted butter, melted

1 ounce apple brandy, such as Applejack (optional)

12 large Granny Smith apples (3¼ to 3½ pounds), peeled, cored, and cut into ¼-inch-thick slices

Hazelnut Crumble Topping

1 cup all-purpose flour

1 cup whole-wheat flour

1 cup packed light brown sugar

1 teaspoon ground cinnamon

16 tablespoons (8 ounces) unsalted butter, cut into pieces and chilled

1 cup hazelnuts, toasted and coarsely chopped

1 pint vanilla ice cream (optional)

1. Preheat the oven to 350°F. Butter a 9 x 13-inch baking dish or other shallow 2-quart baking dish. Set aside.

2. To make the apple filling: Combine the lemon zest and juice, cider, sugar, cinnamon, nutmeg, butter, and brandy, if desired, in a large bowl. Add the apples and toss to coat. Set aside.

3. To make the hazelnut crumble topping: In a medium bowl combine the all-purpose flour, whole-wheat flour, sugar, and cinnamon. Using your fingers, work in the butter until the mixture is crumbly and forms pea-sized lumps. Add the hazelnuts; mix until evenly distributed.

4. Spread the apple mixture in the bottom of the prepared baking dish. Sprinkle the hazelnut crumble evenly over the apples. Bake for 25 minutes, rotate the dish and bake until the top is crisp and golden brown, about 25 more minutes. Let cool for 10 minutes; serve warm with scoops of vanilla ice cream, if desired.

Simon Pearce

THE SILVER FORK RESTAURANT

The Silver Fork is a small, elegant six-table restaurant in Manchester Center that showcases the award-winning cooking skills of Chef Mark French. When he was younger, French trained with a German chef, then worked with international chefs for 10 years, and later lived and cooked in Puerto Rico for 13 years. He incorporates all of these amazing experiences into his cooking style. His international menu is always in "movement" with an emphasis on flavor, freshness, and inspiration. The restaurant offers a full bar and a large selection of wines by the glass that change as frequently as the menu, and are all dedicated to enhancing each meal. With a strong belief in friends, fun, and flavor, the Silver Fork is a unique dining experience.

Bread Pudding Soufflés with Coconut Vanilla Crème Anglaise

SERVES 8

Mark French developed this recipe at the last minute for group of patrons who were eating at the restaurant. He created the dish using only ingredients that were available in his kitchen at the time. You will need a total of 14 eggs for this recipe; reserve two of the leftover whites from the crème anglaise to use in the soufflés.

Crème Anglaise

1 vanilla bean

2 cups heavy cream

2 cups whole milk

1 can cream of coconut, such as Coco Lopez

6 tablespoons granulated sugar

8 large egg yolks, beaten

2 tablespoons cornstarch

Soufflés

Unsalted butter, for soufflé cups

Granulated sugar, for soufflé cups

2 (14-ounce) cans sweetened condensed milk

2 cups milk

6 large eggs, separated, plus 2 large egg whites

1½ teaspoons vanilla extract

1 teaspoon ground cinnamon

1 pound (1 loaf) bread, such as challah, cut into ½-inch cubes

4 bananas, sliced

1 cup raisins

½ cup sliced almonds

Confectioners' sugar

1. To make the crème anglaise: Place the vanilla bean on a work surface and split it in half lengthwise using a paring knife. Scrape the seeds into a large saucepan and add the cream, milk, cream of coconut, and sugar. Bring to a simmer over medium heat.

2. Combine the egg yolks and cornstarch in a large bowl and whisk until pale yellow. While whisking, add ¼ cup of the warm cream mixture. Slowly add the remaining cream, then return the mixture to the saucepan and simmer gently, stirring often, for 15 minutes. Strain the mixture through a fine-mesh strainer and refrigerate until ready to serve.

3. To make the soufflés: Preheat the oven to 350°F. Coat eight 8-ounce soufflé cups or soup cups with butter. Line each cup with granulated sugar and discard any excess.

4. In a large bowl, whisk together the condensed milk, milk, egg yolks, vanilla, and cinnamon. Add the bread, bananas, raisins, and almonds and toss to coat. Beat the egg whites until stiff peaks form and gently fold into the bread mixture.

5. Divide the soufflé mixture among the cups.

6. Bake the soufflés, uncovered, until set and the bread is puffed and lightly browned, 20 to 25 minutes. Unmold the soufflés onto dessert plates, pour some of the crème anglaise on and around each soufflé, dust with confectioners' sugar, and serve.

The Silver Fork Restaurant

ODYSSEY EVENTS

As former successful restaurant managers and co-owners of the renowned Hemingway's Restaurant in Killington, Linda and Ted Fondulas have decades of experience with dining innovations. Forerunners of wine tasting and farm-to-table dinners in Vermont, their history tapping into local ingredients dates to the 1970s.

After restaurants came Newhall Farm and the creation of brand products, such as Newhall Farm Ice Cider. The couple's latest venture includes event planning plus directing hands-on cooking classes at their mountain top idyll in Bridgewater Corners. As always, Linda and Ted still source local products and can't help being hospitality oriented!

Though Puckerbrush Cider Company has taken over cider production at Newhall Farm, Ted and Linda highly recommend you enjoy their ice cider!

Pumpkin Custard

SERVES 6

The custard preparation came about during the fall when Ted and Linda Fondulas were looking for a new seasonal dessert. Lucy Allen, their pastry chef at the time when the couple owned Hemingway's Restaurant, worked out this recipe using fresh pumpkin. Any sugar pumpkin, such as Baby Pam, will work well in this recipe. You will need an electric juicer, such as a Vitamix, for this recipe.

2 (3-pound) baking pumpkins

4 cups half-and-half

1-inch cinnamon stick

2 allspice berries

1-inch vanilla bean

1 teaspoon grated orange zest

½ cup whole milk, or as needed

4 large eggs plus 3 large egg yolks

6 tablespoons granulated sugar

1. Preheat the oven to 325°F. Spray six 6-ounce ramekins with nonstick cooking spray and set aside.

2. Cut the pumpkins in half lengthwise; remove and discard the seeds and strings. Peel the pumpkins, cut them into chunks, and juice them with an electric juicer. Reserve the pulp. Place the pumpkin juice in a medium saucepan over medium heat, and reduce to ½ cup, about 5 minutes. Pour the reduced juice over the reserved pumpkin pulp.

3. In a separate medium saucepan, bring the half-and-half, cinnamon stick, allspice berries, vanilla bean, and orange zest to a simmer over medium-high heat. Pour the mixture over the pumpkin pulp and juice and let stand for 20 minutes.

4. Strain the half-and-half and pumpkin mixture through a fine-mesh strainer into a bowl, pressing firmly to get as much liquid into the bowl as possible, then strain again into a 4-cup liquid measuring cup. (Straining twice is important to remove the starch from the pumpkin.) Add enough whole milk to equal 3 cups. Return the pumpkin mixture to the saucepan and bring to a simmer over medium heat. Let cool.

5. Whisk together the eggs, yolks, and sugar in a medium bowl. Add the pumpkin cream a little at a time, whisking continually. Ladle the mixture into the prepared ramekins. Place the ramekins in a small roasting pan and add enough water to the roasting pan to come halfway up the sides of the ramekins.

6. Bake until the custards are set but still wiggly in the center, 35 to 40 minutes. Remove the ramekins from the roasting pan and refrigerate overnight before serving.

Odyssey Events

Panna Cotta with Maple Aspic

SERVES 6

A rich panna cotta is topped with a light maple aspic layer and subtly flavored with Vermont White and Vermont Gold Vodka, produced by Vermont Spirits. It is truly a serendipitous union; vodkas distilled from the fermentation of milk sugar and maple sap and their natural counterparts, cream and maple syrup. To make a lighter version you may substitute milk or half-and-half for up to 1 cup of the cream.

Panna Cotta

½ cup whole milk

1 packet (about 2½ teaspoons) unflavored gelatin

2 cups heavy cream

½ cup Vermont White vodka

½ cup granulated sugar

2 teaspoons vanilla extract

Maple Aspic

¼ cup water

1 teaspoon unflavored gelatin

½ cup pure Vermont maple syrup

¼ cup Vermont Gold vodka

1. To make the panna cotta: Combine the milk and gelatin in a small bowl. Let sit for 10 minutes.

2. Meanwhile, heat the cream, vodka, and sugar in a large saucepan over medium heat until the mixture almost comes to a boil, stirring until the sugar is dissolved. Add the gelatin mixture and vanilla and gently whisk over low heat until the gelatin is dissolved.

3. Strain the mixture into a heatproof container with a spout and fill six martini glasses about two-thirds full. Transfer to the refrigerator.

4. To make the maple aspic: When the panna cotta has begun to set (after about 30 minutes), combine the water and gelatin in a small bowl. Let sit for 10 minutes.

5. Meanwhile, warm the maple syrup and vodka in a small saucepan over low heat until simmering. Add the gelatin mix and gently whisk until the gelatin has dissolved. Let the mixture cool slightly, then strain it into a container with a spout and let cool completely.

6. Make sure the panna cotta has set enough (jiggle it slightly; it should be firm), then slowly pour the cooled maple mixture over it. Refrigerate for several hours or overnight before serving.

Vanna Guldenschuh for Vermont Spirits

DARBY FARM

Darby Farm, in Alburgh, is a diversified, certified organic family-run operation, which produces strawberries, vegetables, honey, and grains. The farm has been in the Darby family for over 200 years. Heather Darby, a member of the seventh generation of this Vermont farming family, operates the farm with her husband, Ron Hermann. They offer CSA shares in the summertime, along with a farm stand, which is open from May to October.

In 2007, Darby started an apiary on the farm. Her goal was to carry on the legacy of her great grandfather, Aubrey Darby, who was once a prominent beekeeper in Vermont. Today, she has 15 hives, which offer her a great deal of pleasure and relaxation, as well as sweet rewards.

Honey Ice Cream with Fresh Strawberries

SERVES 6

You can adjust the intensity of the honey flavor by modifying the amount used. The sliced strawberries provide a bright counterpoint to the honey's sweetness, but you can omit them, allowing the velvety smooth ice cream to stand on its own.

1 cup whole milk

4 large egg yolks

½–¾ cup Vermont honey

3 cups heavy cream

2 cups sliced strawberries

1. Heat the milk in a medium saucepan over medium-low heat until it just starts to simmer.

2. While the milk is heating, whisk the egg yolks in a medium bowl. Gradually add the hot milk to the egg yolks and whisk to combine. Gently stir in the honey.

3. Return the mixture to the saucepan and cook over medium-low heat, stirring constantly, until the mixture thickens and coats a wooden spoon.

4. Add the heavy cream and stir to combine. Strain the mixture through a fine-mesh strainer into a clean container. Cover with plastic wrap, pressing the plastic directly onto the surface of the mixture, and refrigerate overnight.

5. Pour the ice cream mixture into an ice cream maker and freeze according to the manufacturer's directions. Scoop the ice cream into bowls and top each serving with ⅓ cup sliced strawberries.

Darby Farm

Vermont Maple Ice Cream

SERVES 6 TO 8

This rich and creamy ice cream has a beautiful, delicate maple flavor.

4 cups half-and-half

10 large egg yolks

6 tablespoons granulated sugar

1½ cups grade B Vermont maple syrup

1 cup heavy cream

1. Heat the half-and-half in a medium saucepan over low heat until it just starts to simmer.

2. While the half-and-half is heating, whisk together the egg yolks and sugar in a medium bowl until slightly thickened and pale yellow in color. Gradually add the hot half-and-half to the egg yolk mixture and whisk to combine. Gently stir in the maple syrup.

3. Return the mixture to the saucepan and cook over medium-low heat, stirring constantly, until the mixture thickens and coats a wooden spoon. Do not bring mixture to a boil.

4. Add the heavy cream and stir to combine. Strain the mixture through a fine-mesh strainer into a clean container. Cover with plastic wrap, pressing it directly onto the surface of the mixture, and refrigerate overnight.

5. Pour the ice cream mixture into an ice cream maker and freeze according to the manufacturer's directions. Serve.

Jim Gioia and Warren Store

Maple Crème Brûlée

SERVES 4

The flavor of pure Vermont maple syrup is high-lighted in this silky, creamy custard.

2 cups heavy cream

½ teaspoon vanilla extract

3 large eggs plus 1 medium egg, lightly beaten

¼ cup pure Vermont maple syrup, preferably Grade B

2 tablespoons raw cane or turbinado sugar

1. Preheat the oven to 325°F.

2. Bring the heavy cream and vanilla to a simmer in a medium saucepan over medium-high heat. Let cool to lukewarm.

3. In a medium bowl, whisk together the eggs and maple syrup. Add the warm cream a little at a time, whisking continually. Ladle into four 8-ounce broiler-safe ramekins. Place the ramekins in a small roasting pan and add enough water to the roasting pan to come halfway up the sides of the ramekins. Bake until the custard is set but still wiggling in the center, about 40 minutes. Remove the ramekins from the roasting pan and refrigerate for at least 2 hours or up to 3 days.

4. Adjust an oven rack to the top position and heat the broiler. Place the ramekins on a baking sheet and sprinkle the custards with the sugar. Broil until the sugar caramelizes. Serve immediately.

Osborne Family Maple

Tart aux Noix (Walnut Tart)

SERVES 8 TO 10

This elegant tart is simple to make and so delicious! It has a rich buttery caramel filling that pairs beautifully with the slightly bitter tasting walnuts. A dollop of the silky, subtly tart crème fraîche perfectly balances the sweetness of the tart.

Crust

¼ pound unsalted butter, at room temperature

1 egg yolk

2 tablespoons white sugar

1 cup plus 2 tablespoons all-purpose flour

Filling

½ pound walnut halves or pieces (just under 2 cups)

⅔ cup heavy cream

1½ cups white sugar

6 tablespoons water

2 tablespoons brandy, such as BHAKTA 27-07 Brandy

4 tablespoons unsalted butter

Crème fraîche as needed

1. To make the crust: In a large bowl, cut the butter into small pieces. Using two sharp knives, cut in the egg yolk, followed by the 2 tablespoons sugar, then the flour, until it resembles coarse cornmeal. Simply hold the knives parallel to each other and repeatedly cut in opposite directions.

2. When the butter is well coated with flour, using your hands, mix until the dough is no longer sticky and holds together. Form the dough into a smooth ball and let rest for 1 to 2 minutes. Then pat the dough into your 9-inch tart pan, making sure there are no cracks. Do not prick the dough.

continues . . .

3. Place the crust into the refrigerator for at least 1 hour. If using a store-bought pastry, unroll it into your tart pan and refrigerate. This step may be done several hours in advance.

4. When ready to prepare the filling, preheat the oven to 400°F.

5. To toast the walnuts: Line a baking sheet with parchment paper. Scatter the walnuts evenly over the parchment paper and toast for 5 minutes. Set aside to cool. Do not turn off the oven.

6. To make the caramel: Pour the cream into a small saucepan and just warm over low heat until needed for the caramel.

7. Combine the 1½ cups white sugar, water, and brandy and stir until the sugar dissolves over medium heat. Once the sugar has dissolved, do not stir the liquid anymore. Occasionally pick up the saucepan and carefully move it to gently swish the liquid around so that the caramel is heated evenly. Raise the heat and cook until the caramel turns a light golden brown, about 5 minutes. Remove from heat. The caramel will continue to cook and will darken more as it cooks with the cream. During this step, it is important to keep a close eye on the caramel to avoid scorching. The key is being ahead of letting the caramel color get too dark too soon.

8. To make the filling: In a slow and steady stream, pour the warm cream into the hot caramel. If a skin has formed on the cream, use a spoon to remove it first, then stir the cream well before adding the caramel carefully. Stand back; the caramel will bubble. When the bubbling subsides, stir in the butter. Place over medium heat, add the walnuts and cook for 2 minutes, stirring occasionally.

9. Remove the chilled tart shell from the refrigerator and pour in the filling, spreading the nuts out evenly over the surface of the tart shell.

10. Transfer the tart to the oven, turn down the heat to 350°F and bake for about 30 minutes, or until the crust has a nice golden color. Check halfway through to ensure that the walnuts are not cooking too quickly (turning dark). If they are, cover the tart loosely with a sheet of aluminum foil. If the tart is still bubbling when the crust is ready, that's fine. The filling will set as the tart cools.

11. To serve: The tart can be served warm or at room temperature. Top with a dollop of crème fraîche, if desired.

Note: The tart can be made ahead of time and gently reheated just before serving.

Chef Philip Davis for BHAKTA 50 Spirits

SUSANNA'S CATERING, LLC

Susanna Keefer's childhood years were a wonderful combination of adventure and discovery. Born and raised in the south of England, each year her parents would take the family to France to spend a couple of fun-filled weeks. They traveled there on a Scandinavian overnight ferry that hosted a smorgasbord buffet in the evening that consisted of fantastic displays of mouthwatering food. During these excursions, Susanna's parents would allow her to choose whatever she wanted to eat for dinner, if she ate everything that was on her plate.

Those two delightful weeks in France were spent at a beachfront campsite that had a camp kitchen that sold everything from croque monsieurs to steak frites, bouillabaisse and oeufs a la neige. Her parents did most of the cooking while they were there, with Susanna falling in love early on with the dressed crabs that her dad brought back from the market. To this day, that dish elicits happy memories of days gone by.

Susanna's father was a wonderful gardener growing all the vegetables, fruits, and berries that the family needed. Meat was purchased fresh from the butcher shop, milk left on their doorstep by the milkman, and eggs from the local egg farm arrived daily. Both of her parents considered cooking to be an art and encouraged their daughter to help in the kitchen. Fresh was the order of the day and Susanna learned at a young age that eating healthy, nutritious food was the way to live an active, nutrient-rich life.

The busy chef admits, "Cooking is my craft. I have practiced it pretty much daily for almost 40 years and still learn something every time I step into the kitchen. My passion for creating totally balanced meals, while incorporating world spices and local ingredients, continues to deepen.

I guess my culinary philosophy is that cooking has to come from the heart with the knowledge that you are creating something that has the power to give you pleasure, as well as provide the body with all it needs to perform and thrive."

This ideology began to develop in her late teens while working on the hotel barges that ran through the wine districts of La Loire and Bourgogne. The teenager watched and learned while helping the barges' skilled chefs to cook classic French dishes. Traveling along the canals that meandered through villages and towns, Susanna was exposed to the most extraordinary wines and authentic foods, all the time learning more about the cuisine of each area that they visited.

When Susanna returned to the south of France, she had graduated to the position of chef. During

her eight-year career as head chef on luxury, privately owned motor and sailing yachts, she cruised the Mediterranean, Caribbean, and North American waters. The talented chef enjoyed employing different styles of cooking. As her career began to grow, visits to the fresh food markets of the Mediterranean and Caribbean served to spark her creative juices.

Susanna came to the United States to visit a friend in the Stowe area of Vermont and liked the location so much that she ended up staying. She furthered her education and experience by working at several of Stowe's finest restaurants before opening her private chef and catering company in 2003. Her catering business of 18 years uses locally sourced ingredients in its globally inspired dishes, creating superb meals and memorable dining experiences for folks in the Stowe area, and beyond. The busy entrepreneur readily admits that her clients guide her menus and her business growth. Longstanding friendships have flowered during celebrations of births, weddings, memorial services, and countless other memorable occasions. For Susanna, her catering business represents much more than a job. She considers it an honor to be invited into someone's home to help them celebrate a special occasion with a meal that is pleasing to the senses. Knowing that what she has created is not only delicious but nutritious as well, gives her a great sense of accomplishment.

In March 2020, the busy chef launched Susanna's to Go, which provides prepared meals that can be finished at home. This offshoot of the business entails delivering food to the homes of elderly clients and other community residences where folks need support with their dietary needs. Both businesses are in Morrisville, Vermont's lower village, right on the Lamoille Rail Trail. To accommodate the workload for the catering and to-go companies, Susanna employs 3 kitchen staff, 10 to 12 front of house staff, and another 6 on-site.

During June 2020, at the height of the pandemic, the catering company had lost 90 percent of its business and it became clear that traveling would be out of the question for quite some time. Susanna, never one to sit idly by, saw an online course in "Nutrition and Healthy Living" advertised by Cornell University. As her husband suffered from cardiovascular problems, the subject matter immediately piqued her interest and she enrolled in the course. She believed that this course would not only be an asset, but a tool in helping his recovery; educating her about the power of food in avoiding disease. Today, Susanna is very comfortable cooking vegan, gluten-free, low-glycemic meals. The Nutrition and Healthy Living Certificate that she has earned from Cornell University reinforces some of her health claims and has guided her with cooking more diet specific meals which benefit many of her clients. This incredible course has been life changing for both Susanna and her husband.

The busy chef's loyalty and support extend to the local farming community as well. She strongly believes that the quality of product, humanity, talent, and incredible work ethic of local farmers must be supported and sustained if we are to survive. As she notes, "My whole life I have searched out the real food sources, working with our local farmers and purveyors is the most rewarding relationship that I could ask for." Susanna totally relies on the local farmers that she uses to provide her business with the freshest, highest quality produce and products that are available. In return, she supports these folks and their businesses by spreading the word and emphasizing the quality of their products to her clients, a win-win situation for all. Even though both of Susanna's companies

do not offer alcohol to clients, it is sometimes used in her recipes, supporting local distillers.

For Susanna Keefer, Vermont's small businesses and the products that they produce exemplify a commitment to quality and customer service that stands head and shoulders above the rest. It is this unwavering dedication that these folks are most proud of. Susanna stands out as a shining example of these values, having been awarded Vermont Business Magazine's 2017 Best of Business Award for her catering company. This award acknowledged her as "Best Corporate Event Caterer in the Central Vermont/Northeast Region," a well-deserved honor.

The hardworking, creative chef continues to shine with her Mama Hoo-Rah dip, which is available in specialty grocery stores and markets across Vermont. This saucy, spreadable dip is gluten-free and vegan. Because of its versatility, it has become very popular as a dip, spread, or sauce which can be used for pizza or with pasta. The roasted red pepper base and mix of spices give it some kick while ground walnuts, pomegranate molasses and maple syrup prevent the heat from being overwhelming. Puréed white beans give it a smooth texture. Mama Hoo-Rah is thick enough to cling to vegetables, tortilla chips, or sliced apples and is equally as yummy brushed on meat, fish, or vegetables when grilling. Susanna took the name from the Arabic "hoo-rah," a type of Middle Eastern celebratory dance. Her goal was to create something fun, playful, and healthy.

Susanna Keefer learned early on in her culinary and catering career that the business relationships we form, and the strength and support which is given to each other through these connections, is what makes Vermont truly unique. The state has an unmatched reputation and brand created by the folks that live there and the small businesses that call it home. She is thankful to live and work in such a special place. It is with immense pride that this talented chef calls the Green Mountain State home.

Vermont Maple, Apple, and Brandy Tarte Tatin with Lavender Whipped Cream

SERVES 8

This delicious upside-down apple tart is a classic recipe of French cuisine. The apples are so soft and luscious with a lovely dark color. The crust has just the right amount of firm resistance in the bite and the lavender whipped cream is a decadent addition. See photos on pages 217 and 219.

Lavender Whipped Cream

1½ cups heavy whipping cream

3 tablespoons Vermont honey

½ tablespoon dried lavender blossoms

Pastry Dough

1½ cups all-purpose flour

6 tablespoons powdered sugar

Pinch of fine-grain sea salt

10 tablespoons (1¼ sticks) cold unsalted butter, cut into small pieces

2 tablespoons ice water

Tarte Tatin Filling

3 pounds firm-fleshed apples (about 6 to 7 large apples), preferably Granny Smith or Honeycrisp

1 tablespoon fresh lemon juice

4 tablespoons (½ stick) butter

½ cup light brown sugar

¼ cup Vermont grade-B maple syrup

2 tablespoons apple brandy, such as Mad River Distillers or Dead Bird Brandy

1. To make the lavender cream: Combine the cream, honey, and lavender in a small saucepan and bring to a gentle simmer over medium-high heat, stirring occasionally, about 5 minutes. Do not let the cream come to a boil. Remove from the heat and allow to steep, covered, for 40 minutes. Strain through a cheesecloth-lined fine-mesh strainer into a medium bowl. Gather the corners of the cheesecloth and gently squeeze out any excess cream into the bowl, discarding or composting the plant matter. Cover with plastic wrap, and transfer to the refrigerator and let chill for at least 4 hours. Before you plan to make the whipped cream, place a metal mixing bowl and metal whisk attachments from a handheld mixer into the freezer for about 15 minutes.

2. To make the pastry dough: Place the flour and sugar in the bowl of a food processor and pulse until just combined. Scatter the butter pieces over the flour mixture and cut into the flour with pulses until it resembles coarse cornmeal. While the machine is running, add the water until the dough comes together. Place the dough on a floured work surface and flatten into a ½-inch disc.

3. Place a piece of parchment paper the size of a baking sheet near your work area. Dust your rolling pin with flour. Roll out the dough into an ⅛-inch thickness and 2 inches larger than the diameter of the cast-iron skillet on the parchment paper. Place an 11-inch plate upside down on the rolled-out dough. Using a sharp knife, cut a circle around the plate. Roll the dough circle and parchment paper onto the floured rolling pin and gently unroll on the parchment paper side down onto the baking sheet. Transfer to the refrigerator and allow to chill until ready to use.

4. To prepare the apples: Peel the apples, slice them into quarters, and remove the core. Place the apples in a large bowl and toss with the lemon juice. Set aside.

5. Preheat the oven to 350°F.

6. To make the Tarte Tatin filling: Combine the butter, sugar, maple syrup, and apple brandy in a 10-inch cast-iron skillet and cook over medium-low heat, swirling the mixture in the skillet frequently until the sugar dissolves and the mixture starts to bubble, about 9 minutes. Immediately remove from the heat and set aside.

7. Starting in the center of the skillet, carefully arrange the apples, flat side down, in concentric circles, making sure to pack them tightly.

8. Return the skillet to the stovetop and over medium-low heat, bring the syrup mixture to a boil, about 3 minutes. Cover the skillet and cook for 5 minutes. Uncover, and continue to cook until the sauce thickens and turns an amber caramel color. Remove from the heat and set aside.

9. Remove the dough from the refrigerator and gently lay the dough and parchment paper dough side down over the top of the tatin, then slowly peel back the parchment paper, leaving the dough behind. Carefully tuck the edges of the dough in between the apples and the edge of the skillet. Be careful not to touch the hot liquid. Place the skillet on a baking sheet and transfer to the oven and bake for about 35 minutes or until the crust is firm and the skillet juices are bubbling.

10. Remove from the oven and let stand on a cooling rack for 10 minutes. While the tart is resting, make the lavender whipped cream. Remove the metal mixing bowl and whisks from the freezer. Place the lavender-infused cream into the chilled bowl, then whisk on medium-high speed, scraping down the sides of the bowl as needed, until medium peaks form.

11. To assemble: Carefully run a sharp knife around the edge of the skillet to loosen the tart. Quickly and carefully, invert onto a platter that is at least 2 inches larger than the diameter of the cast-iron skillet. If any of the apples remain in the skillet, gently use a spatula to remove them and carefully arrange them on the tart.

12. To serve: Cut into wedges and serve warm with a dollop of lavender whipped cream.

Note: The tart can be stored in an airtight container at room temperature for up to 2 days. The pastry dough can be made by hand if you don't own a food processor. Gently run the flour covered butter pieces repeatedly between your fingers and thumbs until it resembles coarse cornmeal, then add the 2 tablespoons of water, and again using your hands mix until the dough comes together and forms a ball.

Susanna's Catering, LLC

DIRECTORY

A

American Flatbread Company
Lareau Farm
46 Lareau Road
Waitsfield, VT 05673
Email: George@americanflatbread.com
Telephone: 802-496-8856
Website: www.americanflatbread.com

Appalachian Gap Distillery
88 Mainelli Road
Middlebury, VT 05753
Telephone: 802-989-7362
Website: www.appalachiangap.com

Arcana Gardens and Greenhouses
175 Schillhammer Road
Jericho, VT 05465-3045
Telephone: 802-899-5123
Website: www.arcanagardens.com

B

The Bakery at the Farmhouse Kitchen
377 Pine Street
Burlington, Vermont 05401
Telephone: 802-862-5524

Bhakta 50 Spirits
1 Brennan Circle
Poultney, VT 05764
Telephone: 802-287-8340
Website: www.bhaktaspirits.com

Blue Ledge Farm
2001 Old Jerusalem Road
Salisbury, VT 05769
Email: info@blueledgefarm.com
Telephone: 802-247-0095
Website: www.blueledgefarm.com

Boyden Valley Winery & Spirits
64 Vermont Route 104
Cambridge, VT 05444
Email: info@boydenvalley.com
Telephone: 802-644-8151
Website: www.boydenvalley.com

Burlington Farmers' Market
P.O. Box 4117
Burlington, VT 05406
Email: burlingtonfarmersmarket.org@
    gmail.com
Telephone: 802-560-5904
Website: www.burlingtonfarmersmarket
    .org

Butterfly Bakery of Vermont
698 South Barre Road
Barre, VT 05641
Email: orders@ButterflyBakeryVT.com
Telephone: 802-243-4545
Website: butterflybakeryvt.com

Butterworks Farm
421 Trumpass Road
Westfield, VT 05874
Email: orders@butterworksfarm.com
Telephone: 802-744-6855
Website: www.butterworksfarm.com

C

Cabot Creamery Co-operative
193 Home Farm Way
Waitsfield, VT 05673
Email: info@cabotcheese.coop
Telephone: 888-792-2268
Website: www.cabotcreamery.com

Café Mamajuana
88 Oak Street
Burlington, VT 05401
Email: maria@cafemamajuana.com
Website: www.cafemamajuana.com

Capital City Farmers Market
P.O. Box 515
Montpelier, VT 05601
Email: manager@montpelierfarmers
    market.com
Telephone: 802-793-8347
Website: capitalcityfarmersmarket.com

Carpenter & Main Restaurant
326 Main Street
P.O. Box 1623
Norwich, VT 05055
Email: carpenterandmain@yahoo.com
Telephone: 802-649-2922
Website: www.carpenterandmain.com

Cedar Circle Farm & Education Center
225 Pavillion Road
East Thetford, VT 05043
Email: growing@cedarcirclefarm.org
Telephone: 802-785-4737
Website: www.cedarcirclefarm.org

City Market, Onion River Cooperative
82 South Winooski Avenue
Burlington, VT 05401
Email: info@citymarket.coop
Telephone: 802-861-9700
Website: www.citymarket.coop

Clear Brook Farm
47 Hidden Valley Road
Shaftsbury, VT 05262
Email: Andrew@clearbrookfarm.com
Telephone: 802-442-4273
Website: www.clearbrookfarm.com

Cloudland Farm
1101 Cloudland Road
Woodstock, VT 05091
Email: cloudlandvt@gmail.com
Telephone: 802-457-2599
Website: www.cloudlandfarm.com

Conant's Riverside Farm
2258 West Main Street
Richmond, VT 05477
Email: riverside@gmavt.net
Telephone: 802-434-2588
Website: www.conantsweetcorn.com

Consider Bardwell Farm
1333 Vermont 153
West Pawlet, VT 05775
Email: angela@considerbardwellfarm.net
Telephone: 802-645-0932
Website: www.considerbardwellfarm.com

Courtney Contos
Website: www.ccontos.com

D

Daily Chocolate
7 Green Street
Vergennes, VT 05491-1363
Email: dailychocolatevt@gmail.com
Telephone: 802-877-0087
Website: www.dailychocolateVT.com

Darby Farm
54 North Main Street
Alburgh, VT 05440
Email: darbyfarm@faripoint.net
Telephone: 802-796-3105
Website: www.darbyfarm.com

E

Earth Sky Time Community Farm
1547 Main Street
Manchester Center, VT 05255
Email: earthskytime@gmail.com
Telephone: 802-384-1400
Website: www.earthskytime.com

Eden Specialty Ciders
150 Main Street
Newport, VT 05855
Email: contact@edenciders.com
Telephone: 802-334-4231
Website: www.edenciders.com

F

Farmer Sue
Email: farmersue000@gmail.com

FlowerPower VT
991 Middlebrook Road
Ferrisburgh, VT 05456
Email: flowerpowervermont@gmail.com
Telephone: 802-877-3476
Website: www.flowerpowervt.com

Foote Brook Farm
641 VT Route 15 W
Johnson, VT 05656
Email: joie@footbrookfarm.com
Telephone: 802-730-3587
Website: www.footebrookfarm.com

Full Moon Farm, Inc.
2083 Gilman Road
Hinesburg, VT 05461
Email: nevittrac@gmail.com
Telephone: 802-598-2036
Website: www.fullmoonfarminc.com

G

The Gleanery
133 Main Street
Putney, VT 05346
Email: ismailthechef@gmail.com
Telephone: 802-387-3052
Website: www.thegleanery.com

Greenfield Highland Beef, LLC
487 Gray Road
Plainfield, VT 05667
Email: greenfield1@myfairpoint.net
Telephone: 802-454-7384
Website: www.greenfieldhighlandbeef.com

Green Mountain Garlic
780 Kneeland Flats Road
Waterbury, VT 05676
Email: info@greenmountaingarlic.com
Telephone: 802-882-8263
Website: www.greenmountaingarlic.com

H

Hermit's Gold Wild Edibles
P.O Box 58
963 Route 214
East Montpelier, VT 05651
Email: colin@colinmccaffrey.com
Telephone: 802-454-1007
Website: www.colinmccaffrey.com/
    hermitsgold.html

High Ridge Meadows Farm
1800 Chelsea Mountain Road
East Randolph, VT 05041-0125
Email: info@highridgemeadowsfarm.com
Telephone: 802-728-9768
Website: www.highridgemeadowsfarm
    .com

Honey Road
156 Church Street
Burlington, VT 05401
Website: honeyroadrestaurant.com
Telephone: 802-497-2145

J

Jasper Hill Farm
884 Garvin Hill Road
Greensboro, VT 05842-8987
Email: info@jasperhillfarm.com
Telephone: 802-533-2566
Website: www.jasperhillfarm.com

Jericho Settlers Farm
22 Barber Farm Road
Jericho, VT 05465
Email: farmers@jerichosettlersfarm.com
Telephone: 802-899-4000
Website: www.jerichosettlersfarm.com

Joe's Kitchen at Screamin' Ridge Farm
57 Maple Lane
Montpelier, VT 05602
Email: kitchen@screaminridgefarm.com
Telephone: 802-223-1130
Website: www.screaminridgefarm.com

K

King Arthur Baking Company
135 Route 5 South
Norwich, VT 05055
Email: Jeffrey.hamelman@kingarthurflour
    .com
Telephone: 802-526-1870
Website: www.kingarthurflour.com

Knoll Farm
700 Bragg Hill Road
Fayston, VT 05673
Email: helen.whybrow@gmail.com
Telephone: 802-496-5685
Website: www.knollfarm.org

L

Lazy Lady Farm
973 Snyderbrook Road
Westfield, VT 05874
Telephone: 802-744-6365
Email: laini@lazyladyfarm.com
Website: www.lazyladyfarm.net

Ledgenear Farm
2342 Andersonville Road
West Glover, VT 05875
Email: info@ledgenearfarm.com
Telephone: 802-525-9881
Website: www.ledgenearfarm.com

M

Maplebrook Farm
441 Water Street
North Bennington, VT 05257
Email: info@maplebrookvt.com
Telephone: 802-440-9950
Website: www.maplebrookvt.com

Misery Loves Co.
46 Main Street
Winooski, VT 05404
Email: aaron@miserylovescovt.com
Telephone: 802-825-1910
Website: www.miserylovescovt.com

Misty Knoll Farm
1685 Main Street
New Haven, VT 05472
Email: mistyknollfarm@gmavt.net
Telephone: 802-453-4748
Website: www.mistyknollfarms.com

Moon and Stars Arepas
225 Pavillion Road
East Thetford, VT 05042
Telephone: 802-763-0747
Website: www.moonandstarsvt.org

Mt. Mansfield Creamery
730 Bliss Hill Road
Morrisville, VT 05661
Email: mtmansfieldcreamery@gmail.com
Telephone: 802-888-7686
Website: www.mtmansfieldcreamery.com

N

New Leaf Organics
45 Mountain Terrace
Bristol, VT 05443
Email: newleaf@gmavt.net
Telephone: 802-349-7369
Website: www.newleaforganics.org

O

Odyssey Events
276 Laber Road
Bridgewater Corners, VT 05035
Website: www.odysseyeventsvt.com

Osborne Family Maple, LLC
896 Charleston Road
Island Pond, VT 05846
Telephone: 802-793-6318
Website: www.osbornemaple.com

P

Pebble Brook Farm
188 Menard Road
West Braintree, VT 05060
Telephone: 802-595-0656
Website: www.pebblebrookfarmvt.com

The Pitcher Inn
275 Main Street
Warren, VT 05674
Telephone: 802-496-6350
Website: www.pitcherinn.com

Pitchfork Farm
282 Intervale Road
Burlington, VT 05401
Email: pitchforkfarmvt@gmail.com
Telephone: 802-233-6445
Website: www.pitchforkfarmvt.com

Pomykala Farm
197 East Shore Road N
Grand Isle, VT 05458
Email: info@pomykalafarm.com
Telephone: 802-372-1882
Website: www.pomykalafarm.com

Poorhouse Pies
419 Vermount Route 15
Underhill, VT 05489
Telephone: 802-858-9129
Website: www.poorhousepies.com

Preston's Restaurant at Killington Resort
228 E Mountain Road
Killington, VT 05751
Website: killington.com/prestons-menus

R

River Berry Farm
191 Goose Pond Road
Fairfax, VT 05454
Email: riverberryfarm@gmail.com
Telephone: 802-849-6853
Website: www.riverberryfarm.com

Roma's Butchery
5615 VT-14
South Royalton, VT 05068
Email: romasbutcheryvt@gmail.com
Telephone: 802-763-0440
Website: www.romasbutchery.com

S

Saxton's River Distillery
155 Chickering Drive
Brattleboro, VT 05301
Email: sapling@saplingliqueur.com
Telephone: 802-246-1128
Website: www.saxtonsdistillery.com

Scott Farm Orchard
707 Kipling Road
Dummerston, VT 05301
Email: scottfarmvermont@gmail.com
Telephone: 802-254-6868
Website: www.scottfarmvermont.com

Silver Fork Restaurant
48 W Road
Manchester, VT 05254
Email: thesilverfork@yahoo.com
Telephone: 802-768-8444
Website: www.thesilverforkvt.com

Simon Pearce Restaurant
The Mill
1760 Quechee Main Street
Quechee, VT 05059
Telephone: 802-295-1470
Website: www.simonpearce.com

Smugglers' Notch Distillery
5087 Vermont Route 15
Jeffersonville, VT 05464
Telephone: 802-760-0619
Website: www.smugglersnotchdistillery.com

Snug Valley Farm
824 Pumpkin Lane
East Hardwick, VT 05836
Email: info@snugvalleyfarm.com
Telephone: 802-472-6185
Website: www.snugvalleyfarm.com

Stonewood Farm
105 Griswold Lane
Orwell, VT 05760
Email: stone@stonewoodfarm.com
Telephone: 802-948-2277
Website: www.stonewoodfarm.com

Sterling College
16 Sterling Drive
Craftsbury Common, VT 05827
Website: www.sterlingcollege.edu

Sugarbush Resort
1840 Sugarbush Access Road
Warren, VT 05674
Telephone: 802-583-6311
Website: www.sugarbush.com

Sunshine Valley Berry Farm
129 Ranger Road
Rochester, VT 05767
Email: patricia@vermontberries.com
Telephone: 802-767-9385 (home/office)
   or 802-767-3989 (farm)
Website: www.vermontberries.com

Susanna's Catering
120 Pleasant Street
Morrisville, VT 05661
Telephone: 802-730-3634
Website: www.susannastogo.com

Square Deal Farm
362 Woodward Road
Walden, VT 05843-7034
Email: ray@squaredealfarm.org
Telephone: 802-563-2441
Website: www.squaredealfarm.org

T

Thistle Hill Farm
107 Clifford Road
North Pomfret, VT 05053
Email: info@thistlehillfarm.com
Telephone: 802-457-9349
Website: www.thistlehillfarm.com

T.J. Buckley's Uptown Dining
132 Elliot Street
Brattleboro, VT 05301
Email: TJBuckleys@gmail.com
Telephone: 802-257-4922
Website: www.tjbuckleysuptowndining
   .com

Tracey Medeiros
Website: www.traceymedeiros.com

Twin Farms
452 Royalton Turnpike
Barnard, VT 05031
Telephone: 866-991-8178
Email: info@twinfarms.com
Website: www.twinfarms.com

Two Black Sheep Farm
142 Ferry Road
South Hero, VT 05486
Email: hello@twoblacksheepcsa
   .com
Telephone: 612-309-0896

The Tyler Place Family Resort
P.O. Box 254
Highgate Springs, VT 05460
Email: jeff@tylerplace.com
Telephone: 802-868-4000
Website: www.tylerplace.com

V

Valley Dream Farm, LLC
5901 Pleasant Valley Road
Cambridge, VT 05444
Email: valleydream@wildblue.net
Telephone: 802-644-6598
Website: www.valleydreamfarm.com

Vermont Cranberry Company
2563 North Road
East Fairfield, VT 05448
Email: bob@vermontcranberry.com
Telephone: 802-363-3631
Website: www.vermontcranberry.com

Vermont Salumi
159 N Main Street
Barre, VT 05641
Email: pete@vermontsalumi.com
Telephone: 802-661-8964
Website: www.vermontsalumi.com

Vermont Spirits Distilling Co.
5573 Woodstock Road (on Route 4)
Quechee, VT 05001
Email: info@vermontspirits.com
Telephone: 802-281-6398
Website: www.vermontspirits.com

W

Warren Store
284 Main Street
Warren, VT 05674
Telephone: 802-496-3864
Website: www.warrenstore.com

West Mountain Inn
144 West Mountain Inn Road
Arlington, VT 05250
Email: info@westmountaininn.com
Telephone: 802-375-6516
Website: www.westmountaininn.com

WhistlePig Whiskey
WhistlePig Farm
2139 Quiet Valley Road
Shoreham, VT 05770
Email: info@whistlepigrye.com
Telephone: 802-897-7700
Website: www.whistlepigwhiskey.com

Woodstock Farmers Market
979 West Woodstock Road
Woodstock, VT 05091
Email: mail@woodstockfarmersmarket.com
Telephone: 802-457-3658 ext. 228
Website: www.woodstockfarmersmarket
.com

INDEX

Italics indicate illustrations.

C